The Love That Moves The Sun

The Love That Moves The Sun

Advent hope in a time of crisis

Paul Dominiak

CANTERBURY
PRESS
Norwich

© Paul Dominiak 2024

Published in 2024 by Canterbury Press
Editorial office
3rd Floor, Invicta House,
110 Golden Lane
London EC1Y 0TG, UK
www.canterburypress.co.uk

Canterbury Press is an imprint of Hymns Ancient & Modern Ltd
(a registered charity)

Hymns Ancient & Modern® is a registered trademark of
Hymns Ancient & Modern Ltd
13A Hellesdon Park Road, Norwich,
Norfolk NR6 5DR, UK

British Library Cataloguing in Publication data

A catalogue record for this book is available
from the British Library

ISBN 978-1-78622-565-8

Typeset by Regent Typesetting

For Simeon Paul Raphael

'The only joy in the world is to begin.'

(Cesare Pavese)

Contents

Introduction: Endings

But my desire and will were moved already – like
a wheel revolving uniformly – by
the Love that moves the sun and the other stars.
(Dante Alighieri, *Paradiso*, 33.143–5)[1]

We do well to begin at our end. Our ends form who we are, what we cherish, where we find our joy, and how we act. This book retrieves the ancient but nearly lost sacred art of contemplating the four last things at the end of time: death, judgement, hell and heaven. It retrieves this sacred art as a timely form of contemplation for a contemporary era of compound crises.

Beginning at the end used to be at the heart of the Christian faith.

As it emerged, Christianity was oriented to the last things, called the *eschata* in biblical Greek. In calling Jesus the Messiah, his first followers saw him as God's Anointed, the Chosen One, promised in the Hebrew Scriptures who would reorder the world marred by pain and sin, bringing in God's rule for all ages on the final 'day of the Lord'. As Jesus began his ministry, he proclaimed that he was the one anointed by the Spirit of the Lord. He fulfilled Isaiah's prophecy of the Chosen One who would bring good news to the poor, proclaim release to the captives and recovery of sight to the blind, 'let the oppressed go free', and 'proclaim the year of the Lord's favour' (Luke 4.18–19, quoting Isa. 61.1, 2). Through the teachings, person and work of Christ, Christianity was thoroughly eschatological, meaning it was ordered to the last things of the kingdom of God.

In Jesus' teachings, the kingdom of God that he heralded had a 'now but not yet' quality. Jesus taught his early followers that 'the kingdom of God is within you', sometimes rendered as 'the kingdom of God is among you' (Luke 17.21). He also taught that the kingdom was yet to come. He taught his followers to pray for its coming (Matt. 6.10; Luke 11.2). He said that it was near (Mark 1.15; Matt. 4.17; Luke 10.9, 11). He spoke of the 'last day' when his saving work would be completed (John 6.39–54; 12.44–50). In Jesus, the kingdom of God had been sown but its fullness was still to flower. Believers tasted it and shared in the Holy Spirit (Heb. 6.4). Creation groaned with the labour pains of its birth (Rom. 8.18–25).

The early Christians kept their eyes fixed on the end and prepared for it daily from the beginning. They knew 'neither the day nor the hour' when Christ would return to fulfil the kingdom of God (Mark 13.33; Matt. 25.13; Luke 21.36). They prayed *maranatha*, an Aramaic word meaning 'come, Lord!' (1 Cor. 16.22). *Maranatha* became a sacred word in early Christian worship, and is recorded in the *Didache*, an early handbook composed even before some of the New Testament writings. In anticipation of the end, Christians developed practices to keep them alert. The Desert Father John Cassian commended unceasing prayer of a verse from Psalm 70: 'O God make speed to save me/O Lord make haste to help me.' St Benedict adopted this verse as the opening of daily prayers, a place it still occupies in many versions today. Over the centuries, the last things suffused Christian prayer and practice. St Philip Neri instructed, for example, that 'beginners in religion ought to exercise themselves principally in meditation on the four last things'.[2] Christians lived in the daily awareness that 'all of us must appear before the judgement seat of Christ, so that each may receive recompense for what has been done in the body, whether good or evil' (2 Cor. 5.10).

By the medieval period, the four weeks of Advent that begin the annual cycle of church seasons involved Christians intensely meditating upon the four last things. Medieval priests offered sermons on them. Readings from the Scriptures attended to them, especially to judgement. Hymns sang of the return of Christ at the end of the ages. More broadly, theologians through the centuries reflected upon the last things collectively. Artists vividly depicted them. Poets envisaged the journey of the soul through life, death, judgement, hell and heaven. The last things were the focus of the Christian imagination. The sense of an ending shaped the sense of the present world. Through the sacred art of contemplating death, judgement, hell and heaven, Christians daily parsed the meaning of who they were, what they treasured, where their joy was, and how they ought to live in view of the world to come.

Advent was a particularly well-suited season for the heightened practice of this sacred art. The word 'Advent' comes from a Latin root that means 'coming' or 'arrival'. The season of Advent traditionally spoke of the three comings of Christ who was, would return, and was always present every day through the Holy Spirit. Facing the past, Advent prepared believers for the annual celebration at Christmas of the first coming of Jesus Christ, born as a baby in a manger in Bethlehem. Facing the future, Advent prepared believers for the second coming of Jesus Christ at the end of time. Facing inwards, Advent disclosed how Christ entered Christian hearts daily. Both looking back and looking ahead oriented believers to the way that Jesus shaped them in the present. The season of Advent attended to the disruptive entry of Jesus into everyday lives, begun in his birth and stretching towards the end of time. It reminded believers that their end was to 'live, as it were, the life of God', as the sixteenth-century Anglican theologian Richard Hooker put it.[3]

Christians clearly saw, then, that the singular work of life was to contemplate the last things, from their beginning until their end. This sacred art of contemplating them was both for the season of Advent and for the everyday practice of faith. It lived out the article of faith in the Nicene Creed that proclaimed that Jesus 'will come again in glory to judge the living and the dead, and his kingdom will have no end'. The goal or end of the Christian life was quite simply union with God in the endless kingdom of God inaugurated by Christ in his first coming. This end was final and absolute. 'Our heart is restless until it rests in you,' the North African theologian St Augustine of Hippo prayed to God.[4] For Christians, only by sharing in the life of God through Jesus could human beings finally know who they were, what the fullness of life was, and how they should live. Any other end would not satisfy and would leave the human soul restive. Christians were shaped by the end which drew them to rest in God for all time at the end of the ages.

Contemplating the four last things has suffered almost terminal decline in more recent times. Vestiges of it remain in descriptions of Advent, in special events such as Advent carol services, and in academic theology. It is rare, however, to find ministers who preach on the four last things.

Even more uncommon are Christians who see the four last things as integral to their daily faith or practice. Advent is more typically marked both within and outside the Church by preparing for the celebration of Christ's birth. Believers are more likely to be familiar with lighting a candle on an Advent wreath linked to scriptural readings that revolve around those in both the Hebrew Scriptures and the New Testament who foretold and prepared the way for the birth of Jesus. Eyes look backwards, but not forwards. The last things and the change they inspire receive scant attention. Christingle services and Christmas carols creep in earlier and earlier before Christmas Day, fading the season of Advent into the backdrop of extended Christmas revelry. Outside churches, the glare of lights, buzz of shops, whirr of online orders and blare of seasonal pop music drown out the season of Advent almost completely. Advent calendars are perhaps the only seasonal remnant left in popular practice, and even they mostly have little or no religious content. Contemplating the last things has shrunk to a minor note, and one that is perhaps not even heard at all.

The reasons for this decline are complex. Having a grasp of the decline orients us, however, as to why they are worth retrieving now.

The tenor of the last things in the Christian imagination moved between two tendencies across history, related to the contexts in which believers variously found themselves. It will be the first tendency which this book will revive, and to which we will return later in this introduction.

The early Christians faced perpetual crisis. As a religious minority, they were persecuted and vilified. Oppression was met with vivid apocalyptic visions of triumph over evil, freedom and divine peace. The first tendency, then, was to see the last things as disrupting the status quo in which Christians found themselves, immersed in calamity. They offered a vision of hope in times of crisis where optimism was scarce.

The early Christians imbibed this first tendency from the Hebrew Scriptures and New Testament. In both, times of crisis gave birth to dramatic themes of judgement and the turning over of the world order through the initiative of God. The 'end times' were cosmic in scope and political in character. The tone was apocalyptic, coming from a Greek word meaning 'unveiling' (*apokalupsis*). What was 'unveiled' was the divine rupture of history.

The strongest examples are seen in the books of Daniel and Revelation. The former was probably written during the Syrian-Greek persecution of Jews in the second century BCE but harked back to the forced deportation of Jews in the Babylonian Empire of the sixth century BCE. In these experiences of exile, alienation and injustice, apocalyptic literature expressed a longing for an alternative way. Daniel's apocalyptic visions offered through the last things a way of speaking hope for a different future, of saying 'happy are those who persevere' (Dan. 12.12). Similarly, the book of Revelation emerged in a period of violent persecution for early Christians by the Roman Empire, notably during the infamous reigns of Nero and Domitian. Like Daniel, the visions of Revelation drew upon the last things to envisage a radically different future and a promise that God is 'coming soon' (Rev. 20.7). The apocalyptic imagination of the last things forged in the fires of empire gave a vision of hope amid crisis, a way of seeing the disruptive entry of God into the present.

Once Christianity slowly became allied with political power, however, a second tendency took over. Christians largely no longer faced persecution or oppression, even if there were other crises that they encountered. Over time, they became settled and comfortable. Christianity promoted the peace and order that offered it protection. In later centuries, the Christian imagination focused on the next world rather than this. Christians detailed eternal rewards for moral and civic obedience and infernal punishments for their perceived contraries. The tendency now was to see the last things as referring to some future, otherworldly state. The Scriptures were scoured for ethereal references and often combined with non-biblical influences. The last things became separate from the here-and-now, even if they continued to project the human fears and hopes of the present on to eternity. They encouraged an obedient life of moral rectitude for a future prize, rather than a disruptive vision of hope for the present.

These two tendencies uncomfortably vied with one another in Christian communities over the ages and contributed to the slow but steady decline of the sacred art of contemplating the last things.

At times, such contemplation still erupted in radical ways inspired by the first apocalyptic tendency. Other Christians found such radicalism subversive and needing strict (even violent) control. For example, the Protestant Reformation of the sixteenth century saw radical Christian groups emerge, formed by a sense that the world was being turned upside down and that Christ would imminently return. In the 1530s, following several peasant revolts inspired by the Reformation, a group of reformers took control of the German town of Münster. Fuelled by apocalyptic preaching, they hailed the town as a 'New Jerusalem' preparing for the return of Christ. The reality of this 'New Jerusalem' shocked even other religious dissidents like Martin Luther, the famous founding father of the Reformation movement. Everyone was forced to be re-baptized. Property and goods were held in common. Polygamy was legalized. Sacred artefacts were destroyed. The reaction against Münster was fierce. The town was attacked and the leaders of the city executed, their corpses hung in iron cages from a church steeple as a warning to the people. Memories were long.

Such traumatic episodes rendered the last things suspicious and dangerous, even in some Christian minds.

The Enlightenment heightened this suspicion of the traditional last things. This European intellectual movement in the late seventeenth and early eighteenth centuries privileged reason over tradition, calling into question all received beliefs and practices. The clarion call of this sensibility was sounded by the German philosopher Immanuel Kant's famous maxim, 'dare to know'. For Enlightenment thinkers, the last things were ignorant superstitions, vestiges of irrational traditions devoid of rational basis. It was a moral responsibility to question everything and to seek a secure and reasoned ground for human conduct.

Enlightenment figures first relegated, then rejected, the last things within rational philosophy. Immanuel Kant, for example, framed the last things merely as 'a way of making sensible' the idea of an ultimate moral judgement that underpinned practical reasoning about morality. Others were more critical. For the nineteenth-century German philosopher Ludwig Feuerbach, talk of heaven and hell was no more than a projection of human desire for immortality. Feuerbach's project was to uncover the 'true or anthropological essence of religion'. His work inspired the thinkers whom the twentieth-century French philosopher Paul Ricœur called the 'masters of suspicion' – Karl Marx, Friedrich Nietzsche and Sigmund Freud.[5] These 'masters of suspicion' rejected religion, explaining religious beliefs as an illusory product of human longing. They offered different ways in which human beings could find earthly liberation from that which oppressed them. In effect, the 'masters of suspicion' offered an alternative salvation story, suited to a secular age.

Put together, we can see that, by the nineteenth century, the traditional last things were often seen as dangerous, irrational, illusory and the enemy of human progress.

Roman Catholicism largely insulated itself from these critical challenges of modernity until the mid-twentieth century, and continued the traditional teachings of the last things. Theologians in other traditions, however, transformed their account of the last things because of modern critiques.

Liberal theology emerged out of late-eighteenth-century Protestant attempts to reconfigure traditional Christian teaching in the light of modern understanding and the critique of the last things. Liberal theologians moved away from talking about the rewards and punishments of heaven and hell. The traditional understanding of the last things seemed unpalatable and implausible. Instead, liberal theology saw them as concerning the current movement of history towards moral progress and social perfection. They were brought down to earth and shorn of radical and apocalyptic overtones, resulting in a sanitized and domesticated version of the second historical tendency already described. Liberal theology linked the last things with ethical and civic virtue. Jesus became a moral teacher who taught about a kingdom of God that would be brought about by human effort. The father of liberal theology, Friedrich Schleiermacher, for example, reduced the last things to the process of spiritual growth and progression in religious communities. In a similar vein, the influential Lutheran theologian Albrecht Ritschl viewed the kingdom of God as a realm of moral values into which society was evolving. This liberal theology focused on an optimistic appraisal of human nature, moral growth and social progress. It stressed an easy continuity between this world and the future envisioned by the last things.

The horrors of the First World War shattered the positive worldview of liberal theology. As a result, the last things seemed destined to be consigned to a minor, contested, controversial and exotic note in the melodies of Christian thought. The sacred art of contemplating them was all but left as a superstitious relic of a bygone era.

While we live a long way past these historical events and thinkers, the past still speaks to us. Death, judgement, hell and heaven certainly continue to strike a forbidding and uncomfortable note in the popular imagination. To speak of heaven and hell sounds fantastical and grotesque. To speak of death and judgement sounds morbid and self-righteous. It seems impossible to be a modern person and to contemplate the last things without profound dissonance.

Yet the last things have refused to die. From the early twentieth century onwards, theologians from different traditions have slowly reasserted their central place in Christian thought. Together, they retrieve the first tendency of the early Christians to create a vision of hope, even when crisis and oppression means that optimism about human nature is impossible. This book aims to translate this theological vision of hope into an everyday and accessible sacred art for everyone. It is worth briefly exploring some of the major notes of the theological retrieval of the last things upon which this book will reflect in more detail.

The re-emergence of the last things as a vision of hope began in the time of crisis that seemed to signal their end. As we have seen, the First World War devastated a generation and called into question any optimism about human nature and progress. The surprising reaction of one theologian, however, was not despair but hope. Although the Swiss Reformed theologian Karl Barth had been trained in liberal theology, the First World War shook any confidence he might have had in it. He despaired that many of his teachers had supported the war in the first place. Barth turned from drowsy optimism about human nature to the disruptive hope of Jesus Christ. He developed a 'theology of crisis' in which the hope of Jesus was central.

Barth grasped that Jesus alone, rather than any human process of development, was the 'end of history', meaning its fulfilment. For Barth, the good news of Jesus is 'the fruit of time, the meaning and maturity of history, the fulfilment of prophecy'.[6] Whatever daily personal and collective crises we may encounter, the good news is the crisis that really matters. Barth turned to the Greek root of the word 'crisis' (*krisis*) to explain what he meant. '*Krisis*' means something like 'a decisive time of judgement'. Barth wrote that 'the Gospel of Christ is a shattering disturbance, an assault which brings everything into question'.[7] Jesus confronts us as the 'last thing'. As fully God and fully human, Jesus challenges us to judge everything about us in relation to him.

For Barth, this crisis of the gospel was not cause, however, for angst or despair, even if it is challenging. Jesus is 'the One in whom the Christian is summoned to hope'.[8] Barth repeated time and again that 'Jesus Christ is our hope'.[9] In Christ, we can see that 'God's kingdom is God himself ... as he comes' in Christ.[10] The coming of the 'kingdom of God' in Jesus encounters the world as something entirely new. Barth spoke of the 'kingdom of God' as God's gift – as a 'wholly new order'.[11] The hope that Jesus brings inspires the 'struggle for human righteousness' and the 'revolt against disorder'.[12] Hope in Jesus Christ, then, 'is not an inactive hope' for Barth.[13] It draws believers to share in the unfolding of Christ's saving work to make all things new. It disrupts the status quo. It causes a revolution in lives and opens the vista of new possibility under God.

Barth's theology retrieved the first tendency in early Christian thought to see the last things as speaking into crisis with hope. Other theologians in the twentieth century from different Christian traditions similarly retrieved the last things as a divine principle of rupture that brings a vision of hope amid perpetual human crisis. Two powerful examples of this retrieval are from the Protestant theologian Jürgen Moltmann and from the Roman Catholic Pope Benedict XVI.

Moltmann developed what he called a 'theology of hope' in a book of the same title first published in 1964. Moltmann lived through the crisis of the Second World War, including time as a prisoner of war. While the postwar years brought renewed optimism for many, Moltmann recognized the darker side of secular promises of change, from communism through to fascism and capitalism. He saw their ironic capacity to create despair and oppression rather than freedom. After all, the twentieth century was what the philosopher George Steiner called the 'most bestial in history'.[14] When real hope seemed a rare commodity, Moltmann returned to the last things.

For Moltmann, God's promise to work in the future mattered more than what God had done in the past. He argued that this future should not be seen, however, as far off or as otherworldly. The last things did not announce the arrival of a different world separate from our own. They spoke of the coming future of our reality through the transformation of the present. For Moltmann, the last things meant the 'doctrine of the Christian hope, which embraces both the object hoped for and also the hope inspired by it'.[15] This hope was a 'new heaven and a new earth' born out of the transformation of the present. This hope shines in the crises we face – even despite them. The last things represent 'the glow that suffuses everything here in the dawn of an expected new day'.[16]

Moltmann's 'theology of hope' advocated that Christians must faithfully work to speed the coming of that better world. For Moltmann, the 'theology of hope' involved two other theological virtues – faith and love – first developed by St Paul in the New Testament (1 Thess. 1.3, 5.8; 1 Cor. 13.13). 'Faith, whenever it develops into hope,' wrote Moltmann, 'causes not rest but unrest, not patience but impatience.'[17] The hope of faith issues in love. 'In its hope,' wrote Moltmann, 'love surveys the open possibilities of history. In love, hope brings all things into the light of the promises of God.'[18]

Faced with the same modern cultural context of endless human crisis, Pope Benedict XVI also turned to a vision of hope in his encyclical *Spes salvi*, issued in 2007.[19] The encyclical took its name from Romans 8.24. '*Spes salvi facti sumus*' – in hope we were saved. Like Moltmann, Benedict saw that Christian hope was performative insofar as it shaped the entire Christian life from the perspective of the last things. Like Moltmann, Benedict draws a silver thread that connects faith, hope and love together. Benedict writes that 'faith draws the future into the present' since 'the fact that this future exists changes the present; the present is touched by the future reality'.[20] The vision of the last things as a future reality transforms the view of the believer. 'The dark door of time, of the future, has been thrown open,' writes Benedict. The last things point to the hope of God's promise to remake all things. 'The one who has hope lives differently,' Benedict continues, 'the one who hopes has been granted the gift of a new life.'[21] The source of hope is God's disruptive entry into the messiness of human lives and communities. The 'great true hope which holds firm can only be God – God who has loved us and who continues to love us to the end, until all is accomplished'.[22]

These modern ecumenical retrievals of the early Christian tendency to see the last things as cause for hope in times of crisis show renewed confidence. They embrace death, judgement, hell and heaven as realities that can positively shape the present. They fly contrary to the popular perception of the last things as distasteful relics of the past. Rather, they suggest their integral importance in Christian living. They also point to the disruption they inspire against injustice and suffering as people are caught up into the kingdom of God inaugurated by Jesus and driven forward by the Holy Spirit. Contemplating the last things helps the Christian to grow in grace, which means to grow in the theological virtues of faith, hope and love.

This book builds upon this theological retrieval of the last things witnessed from Karl Barth through to Pope Benedict XVI. It seeks to translate this intellectual retrieval into a form suited to help all Christians redevelop the sacred art of contemplating the last things as part of their daily spirituality and practice of faith.

As we have seen, while at first glance the last things may seem macabre, they are suffused with hope. Hope in Scripture means something like a strong and confident expectation that God's promises for creation will be fulfilled. Even in dark times, hope gives birth to joy. Such joy is not necessarily found in the situation we find ourselves in, but rather in the divine ends to which we are called. With joy comes resilience and fortitude to endure the trials of our present age in the surety of God's action in history. For God is love, we abide in that love through Jesus, and we have faith that God works all things to good in the end.

We sorely need to retrieve the sacred art of contemplating the last things in our daily lives.

As we have seen, in the Scriptures and across the ages, contemplation of the last things gained pertinence at times of crisis. We now live in an age of what some have called a 'polycrisis' or 'permacrisis', meaning extended, multiple and often intersecting crises. In 1992, the American political scientist Francis Fukuyama predicted that the collapse of communism and ascendancy of western liberal democracy and free-market economics signalled the 'end of history'. Fukuyama meant that human development was reaching its final, settled and peaceful form. The past 30 years have seen this to be far from the case.

Human greed and exploitation have caused catastrophic and irreversible environmental harm. We have moved beyond global warming. The world burns. The seas boil. Species perish. We are in a climate crisis and emergency.

The spectre of populism haunts global politics. It feeds on lies and conspiracies. It spreads disinformation. It causes disunity. It sparks wars. We are in a political crisis.

Societies are riven by inequalities around race. Civil rights movements in the twentieth century led to greater equality under law for people of colour, yet they still face inequalities around access to opportunities and outcomes. Racism and racial violence are everyday realities. We are in crisis over racial injustice.

People serve money, and money does not serve people. The classic text of modern economics – Adam Smith's *Wealth of Nations* (1776) – took its title from the vision in Isaiah 60.5 of God's restoration of an exiled and hurt people. Yet modern capitalism has formed what the sociologist Max Weber called an 'iron cage' for all but an elite. It has eroded economic justice. The gap between the 'haves' and 'have nots' grows ever wider. Race, class and gender inequality collide in marketplaces of death. We are in an economic and social crisis around class.

In these (and more) intersecting crises, hope seems in short supply. The possibility of change seems slim. Where once there was optimism, now despair, anger and resignation reign.

The time is propitious, then, to renew the sacred art of contemplating the ends that shape Christian lives. This will enable us to live out St Paul's declaration that 'in hope we are saved' (Rom. 8.24).

As part of this renewal, we need to let go of any tendency to see the last things merely as referring to some imagined future discontinuous with our present.

We need to recapture instead the early Christian tendency to see the last things as disrupting our present. Contemplating our final ends gives a vision of hope in a chaotic world of uncertainty. That vision of hope securely fixes us on Jesus Christ and his coming into our lives.

The first advent began with an angelic messenger announcing the coming of Christ to Mary. Advent calls us to a fresh annunciation of Christ's presence and work in our midst. It calls us to listen to what Jürgen Moltmann called 'the salvation of a groaning creation and the hope of a new earth where justice dwells'.[23]

The following chapters will tackle the four last things in reverse order: heaven, hell, judgement and death. Each chapter links one of the last things with a contemporary crisis to see what might look differently within the sacred art of contemplating the last things. At the end of the book are some questions to aid reflection.

Together, the chapters encourage the development of an 'apocalyptic imagination'.[24] To develop what I mean by this term, it is worth unpacking both words in turn.

We might be used to thinking of the 'apocalypse' as the catastrophic end of the world. The term is popularly used to refer to cataclysmic change brought about by human beings or nature that affects human life and societies.

That is, however, a relatively new understanding of the word. Apocalypse began as a religious way of talking about a once hidden but now revealed divine truth. As we have already seen, the biblical root of the word means an unveiling or a revealing. It is true, of course, that apocalyptic themes of destruction can be found in Jewish, Christian and Islamic texts. Yet God (rather than humanity or nature) is the agent of change. Rather than total catastrophe, the change that God brings involves the radical re-creation or transformation of the existing order. The vision is one of hope that divine justice will reorder all things.

We also might be used to thinking of imagination as something that belongs to the fanciful creation of stories, art and music.

Imagination comes, however, from a Latin root that means something like 'to picture to oneself'. It is the creative and intelligent capacity to see truth. It is a God-given and vital capacity, a distinctly human power that enables us to think beyond the here-and-now and so transform the world in which we live.

The sacred art of contemplating the last things develops an apocalyptic imagination, namely, the creative and intelligent capacity to see and act upon divine truth and a vision of hope for a new future. An apocalyptic imagination is cautiously conditioned by the humbling priority of God's action, rather than our own sense of truth or overweening confidence that we alone have the answers. God uses and expands the human imaginative capacity to see and act. It makes us attend to what Christ unveils about who we are, what we prize, where our joy is, and how we live. Ultimately, an apocalyptic imagination reveals how we can see Christ as the last thing, meaning the endpoint of history. As the Black theologian Brian Bantum writes, 'Christ's birth, life, death, and resurrection performs us and performs upon us, inviting us into a life opened up into the possibility of participation with God.'[25]

An apocalyptic imagination invites us to see and live that kind of life through a vision of hope unveiled in Christ that invites us to 'set your hope on the grace to be brought to you when Jesus Christ is revealed at his coming' (1 Peter 1.13). It guides us to wake up and be alert for the disruptive initiative of God in the here-and-now. Indifference, withdrawal or escapism is not an option. The vision of hope asks us to work with God and within the grain of God's creation – and sometimes against the grain of human societies – to unveil the world as it really is and as it really will be.

Above all else, contemplating the last things reveals God's love at work in and through us. After all, we begin and end with the joy of the divine 'Love that moves the sun and the other stars'.

Notes

1 Dante Alighieri, *The Divine Comedy*, trans. Allen Mandelbaum, New York, London, Toronto: Everyman's Library, 1995, p. 541.

2 Pietro Giacomo Bacci, 'Maxims and sayings' in *The Life of Saint Philip Neri*, London: T. Richardson & Son, 1847, p. 444.

3 Richard Hooker, *The Folger Library Edition of the Works of Richard Hooker*, ed. W. Speed Hill, vols 1–5, Cambridge: Belknap Press, 1977–90, vol. 1, p. 111.

4 Augustine of Hippo, *Confessions*, trans. Henry Chadwick, Oxford: Oxford University Press, 2008, p. 3.

5 Paul Ricœur, *Freud and Philosophy*, trans. Denis Savage, New Haven, CT: Yale University Press, 1970, pp. 33–5.

6 Karl Barth, *The Epistle to the Romans*, Oxford: Oxford University Press, 1933, p. 28.

7 Barth, *Romans*, p. 225.

8 Karl Barth, *Church Dogmatics*, trans. G. W. Bromiley, T. F. Torrance, and others, Edinburgh: T&T Clark, 1936–77, IV/1, p. 116.

9 Karl Barth, *Credo*, trans. J. S. McNab, London: Hodder & Stoughton, 1936, p. 120.

10 Karl Barth, *Christian Life*, trans. G. W. Bromiley, Edinburgh: T&T Clark, 1981, p. 236.

11 Barth, *Church Dogmatics*, III/2, p. 486.

12 Barth, *Christian Life*, pp. 111, 205.

13 Barth, *Church Dogmatics*, IV/4, p. 409.

14 George Steiner, *Errata: An Examined Life*, London: Weidenfeld & Nicolson, 1997, p. 103.

15 Jürgen Moltmann, *The Theology of Hope*, trans. James W. Leitch, New York, NY: Harper & Row, 1967, p. 16.

16 Moltmann, *Theology of Hope*, pp. 15–16.

17 Moltmann, *Theology of Hope*, p. 21.

18 Moltmann, *Theology of Hope*, p. 32.

19 Benedict XVI, *Spes salvi*, 2007, https://www.vatican.va/content/benedict-xvi/en/encyclicals/documents/hf_ben-xvi_enc_20071130_spe-salvi.html, accessed 09.05.2024.

20 Benedict, *Spes salvi*, sects 2 and 7.

21 Benedict, *Spes salvi*, sect. 2.

22 Benedict, *Spes salvi*, sects 27 and 31.

23 Jürgen Moltmann, 'Horizons of Hope', *The Christian Century*, 20 May 2009, pp. 31–3.

24 Richard Bauckham and Trevor Hart, *Hope Against Hope: Christian Eschatology at the Turn of the Millennium*, Cambridge: William B. Eerdmans Publishing, 1999, p. 110, likewise call for 'the primacy of imagination in eschatological thought'.

25 Brian Bantum, *Redeeming Mulatto: A Theology of Race and Christian Hybridity*, Waco, TX: Baylor University Press, 2010, p. 134.

Heaven

'From the days of John the Baptist until now the kingdom of heaven has suffered violence, and the violent take it by force.' (Matthew 11.12)

'Every scribe who has become a disciple in the kingdom of heaven is like the master of a household who brings out of his treasure what is new and what is old.' (Matthew 13.52)

In its profundity I saw – ingathered
and bound by love into one single volume –
what, in the universe, seems separate, scattered.
(Dante Alighieri, *Paradiso*, 33.85–7)[1]

Of the four last things, belief in 'heaven' has proved the most resilient in modern times. In the United Kingdom, while belief in heaven fell from 57 per cent to 41 per cent between 1981 and 2022, this drop was far lower than the decline of religious belief in the same period. In the United States, where religious belief remains more common, 73 per cent of adults surveyed in 2021 expressed belief in heaven. A further 7 per cent believed in some other form of afterlife. In the English idiom, 'heaven' continues to have superlative or euphemistic meanings. It describes how wonderful something is, such as 'this food tastes heavenly'. It also refers to the skies, such as 'the heavens opened' (meaning it rained), or to interstellar sights, such as 'the heavenly constellations' (meaning the stars). 'Heaven' persists in the popular imagination as a source of solace and as a description of the sublime.

The resilience of heaven is not without pressure or problems, however. Two famous pop songs illustrate these pressures and problems: John Lennon's 'Imagine', and Eric Clapton's 'Tears in Heaven'.

In 1971, John Lennon launched the song 'Imagine' in an album of the same name. The song has been consistently listed as one of the greatest, most influential and most played tracks and has been covered by over 200 artists.

'Imagine' has visionary lyrics but remains controversial. The song asks its listeners to imagine what life would be like if there was no heaven and hell, or indeed no religion at all. Lennon invites his listeners to imagine a world without religious, political and economic divisions. For Lennon, these divisions cause war and death. They inhibit the 'brotherhood of man' and the dreamer's hope that 'the world will live as one'.

Lennon stated that 'Imagine' was 'virtually *The Communist Manifesto*', referring to the pamphlet written by Karl Marx and Friedrich Engels in 1848. While Lennon disavowed that he was a communist in the sense it developed in the twentieth century, his reference reveals the core suspicion around heaven. This suspicion puts critical pressure on the idea of heaven. To grasp what that critical pressure is, we need to attend to what the great 'master of suspicion' Karl Marx thought about heaven.

Faced with deep social and economic inequalities in the nineteenth century, Marx turned to consider what prevented positive change. Taking religion into view, he recognized that it was 'the sigh of the oppressed creature, the heart of a heartless world, and the soul of soulless conditions'.[2] Religion expressed real human yearnings for a better world. Yet religion was also 'the opium of the people'. For Marx, the 'last things' of religion deflected people from changing their present condition. Religion preoccupied people with an imagined and otherworldly future promise of heaven and stopped them changing things in the here-and-now.

Marx argued that the traditional last things such as the 'fantastic reality of heaven' were the enemy of political and economic freedom, whereas what mattered was the elimination

of poverty and economic oppression now. He called for workers to take part in a global revolution against the exploitative
capitalism of the Industrial Revolution. Anything – including
religion – that stood in the way of that end was the enemy. The
illusory promise of heaven deferred any action to change the
status quo by imagining some otherworldly resolution of social
ills. 'The abolition of religion as the illusory happiness of the
people', Marx wrote, 'is the demand for their *real* happiness.'[3]

Lennon's 'Imagine' is a popular way of expressing that Marx-
ist criticism of heaven. The enduring popularity of the song
influences the modern suspicion that the idea of heaven may
well be harmful rather than good, an illusion that stunts human
freedom. It calls us to look elsewhere for inspiration for social
change, for unity and purpose in bonds of humanity, separate
from things like religion that divide us.

If the idea of heaven faces this kind of modern critical pressure, then the content of the concept in the popular imagination
also faces problems.

A good cipher for this content is Eric Clapton's song 'Tears
in Heaven'. Clapton composed the song in 1991 following
the tragic death of his four-year-old son, Connor. It topped
numerous charts and received multiple awards. It remains one
of Clapton's best-selling songs. In the song, Clapton wonders
whether his son would know him in heaven, and laments that
he can't be there with him. 'Tears in Heaven' is a moving
tribute to Connor and an iconic ballad about human grief, loss
and longing.

The sentiments of Clapton's song emerged from a wider
popular imagination about what heaven is, itself shaped in
large part by Christianity. As the contemporary British theologian Paula Gooder writes, 'popular attitudes to heaven, while
often hazy and indistinct, revolve around two particular ideas:
that heaven is where we go when we die and that when we get
there the experience will be one of contentment and bliss'.[4]

These popular attitudes are unsurprising given that many
well-known Christian hymns envisage heaven in precisely this
manner. Indeed, powerful currents in the Christian tradition

often suggest the same ideas. 'The kingdom of heaven', wrote St Basil, 'must be contemplation.'[5] Theodoret of Cyrus similarly wrote that 'the way of life in heaven ... is joy and satisfaction, pure and unalloyed'.[6] Heaven belonged 'to the gentle and the mild, to the humble and the unassuming', according to St Leo the Great.[7]

As such, we can see why so many people now see heaven as a spiritual, otherworldly, disembodied reality discontinuous with this world. It seems bound up with the post-mortem fate of individuals, often linked to their innocence or moral worthiness.

While a source of profound consolation, heaven in this sense remains open to the kind of criticism that Marx gave, and which John Lennon sang about. We have pushed heaven into an unknown and spiritual future. We have stymied its power in the here-and-now.

Heaven does not need to be understood, however, in the way it is often imagined and criticized. In the Bible, heaven is rarely seen in the ways we take for granted. Rather than being a place where we go when we die, heaven describes where God dwells, a dwelling integrally linked to the world in which we already live.

If we are to retrieve heaven as part of a sacred art of contemplating the four last things, we must rediscover an apocalyptic imagination about heaven from the Scriptures and the early Christian tradition. This unveils heaven as continuous with this world. It reveals heaven to be pregnant with possibility for the present world. Christ unveils these possibilities so that the 'earth' coincides with 'heaven', just as humanity and divinity coincide in him. The 'kingdom of heaven' describes not so much a place as a community that shares in the life of God. The earth and its peoples are called into such a heavenly reality.

To begin this retrieval, we can start with what the Scriptures say about heaven.

In the Hebrew Scriptures, the word for heaven is *shamayim*. Heaven is not a place of eternal rest and reward for the faithful departed. It refers to the visible sky and to the dwelling place of God. Heaven (*shamayim*) is a created (rather than eternal) reality that exists together with the world. Genesis 1.1 describes how God 'in the beginning ... created the heavens and the earth' as one continuous creation. Hebrew cosmology placed the 'heavens' as 'above' the earth, distinct but related as one creation. This spatial view dominates the Scriptures from Genesis to Revelation. God dwells in the heavens without losing contact with the earth. Angels descend from heaven to earth and ascend back (Gen. 28.12; John 1.51). The Holy Spirit descends from heaven and rests upon Jesus at his baptism (Mark 1.10; Matt. 3.16; Luke 3.22; John 1.32). Jesus ascends back to heaven at the end of his earthly ministry (Mark 16.19; Luke 24.50). Heaven and earth are parts of a created continuum and there is regular commerce between them.

As such 'heaven' and 'earth' were integrally bound together. It makes sense of texts such as Isaiah 66.1, where God declares, 'Heaven is my throne and the earth is my footstool' (quoted in Acts 7.49). Indeed, it explains why 'heaven and earth' regularly appear together in biblical texts. They are distinct but related parts of God's creation. They are also distinct but related parts of God's presence and redemptive activity. The integral wholeness of 'heaven' and 'earth' shaped the mindset of the early followers of Jesus. That is why Revelation 21.1 speaks of a 'new heaven and a new earth' and the passing away of 'the first heaven and the first earth' at the end of time.

We no longer share the Hebrew cosmology that imagines a literal heaven physically located above the earth. We tend to render heaven as an everlasting, distinct and separate spiritual reality. It is an otherworldly destination outside time where people might go when they die. To be fair, elements of this sense of heaven can be found in the Scriptures too. In the New Testament, St Paul at times portrays heaven as the future home of the resurrected believer (2 Cor. 5.1–2). Yet he also portrays heaven as the present dwelling place of Christ from where he will return to finish his transformation of the whole world (Rom. 10.6; 1 Thess. 1.10, 4.16). He strongly encourages a 'now but not yet' character to heaven. Believers are called to be 'citizens of heaven' in the present world as much as in the future (Phil. 3.20).

Although the Hebrew cosmology is no longer scientifically credible, we lose something vital in overly spiritualizing heaven. The basic insight of the biblical idea of heaven is that God dwells alongside and within the earth as its creator and redeemer.

The desire of God to dwell within his creation, seen in the Hebrew language of heaven (*shamayim*), sets the scene for the first coming of Christ. In Christ, the eternal 'Word became flesh and lived among us' (John 1.14). As believers share in Christ, they share in the union of his divine and human natures. God dwells in them. In living the life of God through Christ, believers 'bear the image of the one of heaven' (1 Cor. 15.49). In Jesus, 'heaven' and 'earth' are bound together as one world which he has come to save.

The meaning of heaven and earth coming together in Jesus unfolded in relation to the idea of a kingdom. In his ministry, Jesus talked of the kingdom of God he inaugurated. The kingdom of God translates the biblical Greek phrase *basileia ton Theon*, which occurs over 80 times across the New Testament. The Gospel of Matthew largely prefers the term kingdom of heaven (*basileia ton ouranon*), using it 32 times. While some argue that kingdom of God and kingdom of heaven are different concepts, the majority consensus is that they meant the same thing.

Jesus did not intend this kingdom of God or heaven to refer to some otherworldly place. Neither did he intend it to refer to a kingdom defined by typical human structures of power and privilege. Developing what Jesus meant allows us to begin to develop an apocalyptic imagination as we practise contemplating the last things.

The kingdom of God or heaven begins and ends in Jesus Christ as its ground of reality. It reconfigures right relations within the meeting of heaven and earth where God dwells and where we are called to dwell too. The Hispanic practical theologian Elizabeth Conde-Frazier writes that the kingdom of God is 'neither a territorial realm in the present nor a promised realm that exists only in the future', but rather 'a dynamic in which the power of God is enacted'.[8] Jesus is that power of God unveiled. That power has already erupted into history through him. It is a present but not yet completed reality. As a present reality, the kingdom of God is 'among you' or 'within you' (Luke 17.21). That power will culminate at the end of time in the re-creation of 'heaven and earth' as a new world (Rev. 21.1). It is a final reality yet to come in its fullness. The kingdom of heaven or kingdom of God lingers, waiting for its fulfilment, already close at hand (Mark 1.5; Matt. 3.2; 4.17; 10.7; Luke 10.9, 11; 21.28, 31).

'The kingdom of God' or 'heaven' refers, then, to the mutual indwelling of believers and Christ. As people abide in Jesus, he abides in them. This mutual indwelling transforms the believer such that she is 'conformed to the image' of Jesus (Rom. 8.29) and transformed by love (2 Cor. 3.18). Being 'in Christ' means believers become a 'new creation' (2 Cor. 5.17). Christ is the heart of creation and the substance of the kingdom of heaven. All things 'in heaven and earth' came into being through him (John 1.3; Col. 1.16). All things 'on earth or in heaven' are also reconciled to God through Christ in whom 'all the fullness of God was pleased to dwell' (Col. 1.19–20).

The 'kingdom of God' or 'heaven' also describes the trans-formation of social relations because of this mutual indwelling. It is a divine pledge to honour and re-create all things as they relate to one another. It is the lived social reality of a world transformed by grace. It is the promise of what has broken in through Christ and what God will bring to fulfilment. It is God's 'plan for the fullness of time, to gather up all things in [Christ], things in heaven and things on earth' (Eph. 1.10). Jesus instructed his followers to pray, 'Our Father in heaven, hallowed be your name. Your kingdom come. Your will be done, on earth as it is in heaven' (Matt. 6.9–10). 'Being in Christ' is both individual and communal. That is why so many New Testament images of heaven are communal in nature, portraying it for example as a wedding feast or as a city (Matt. 22.2; Rev. 21.2). As it represents the fullness of life together, heaven is of utmost worth (Matt. 13.44–6).

In the end – in the fullness of time – the kingdom of God or heaven is paradise regained. That paradise is a life of right relations with one another, the whole of creation, and God. That vision of hope is why the Hispanic *mujerista* theologian Ada María Isasi-Diaz, preferred the term 'kin-dom' to 'kingdom'. The word 'kingdom' suggests hierarchy and human power structures, all too prone to inequality, violence and domination. By contrast, 'the word kin-dom makes it clear that when the fullness of God becomes a day-to-day reality in the world at large, we will all be sisters and brothers – kin to each other'.[9] It is 'being in Christ' that forges this new reality of heavenly kinship. The kingdom of heaven is not the music of a distant future. It is the transformative indwelling of Christ.

As we retrieve the scriptural idea of heaven as always related to the earth, we retrieve a vision of hope which sees heaven and earth as bound together in one volume by the divine love that moves the sun and the stars, from start to end. Christ is the beginning and end of that vision of hope in the Christian tradition.

This vision abducts us to see the world in which we live and move in a new light and with a fresh purpose. It is a vision rather than a programme. It does not tell us precisely what to do or how to do it. It unveils God's disruptive activity to draw all things into communion and into union with God. It calls us to attend to God. Waiting, hoping and preparing for God are the roots of human action that flowers in cooperation with God's work already at play.

The kingdom of God or heaven in this sense is not quite a utopia. Utopian accounts typically depict imagined societies of this world with perfect qualities wrought by human work alone. They often give detailed descriptions, and even aspirational aspects to inspire imitation and change. By contrast, the kingdom of God or heaven remains slippery and elusive. It is often couched in terms of parables or in opulent images of a 'new Jerusalem'. Precise detail or prescription is absent. God's action – rather than ours – initiates it. What it means is unpredictable and wild.

Like utopias, however, the kingdom of God or heaven enables an apocalyptic imagination that reveals or unveils the possibility of a different future. As Isasi-Diaz wrote, 'when the present is limiting – oppressive – one looks to the future for a reason for living ... [We] are guided and motivated by our hope for a future in which we can live fully'.[10] The ability to imagine a promised future destroys myths of social inevitability that 'this is just the way things are or have to be'. It refuses a stoic resignation to the iniquities and inequities of the present. It demands that we encounter the strange otherness of the God who disrupts creation with love.

The kingdom of God or heaven is perhaps best described, then, as a 'heterotopia'. The term was developed by the twentieth-century French philosopher Michel Foucault. It combines two Greek words, *heteros* (meaning 'other') and *topos* (meaning 'place'). Foucault's idea of 'heterotopia' describes places and spaces that challenge social norms or expectations. If we expand it to include ideas, then we can see how the kingdom of God or heaven is a heterotopia. It abducts our imagination with the strangeness of God. It disrupts what we may take to be ordinary. It gives a glimpse of an alternative social way of being, still tantalizingly elusive but fertile in its radical possibilities. It is here, now, but not yet completed in its fullness. It compels us to view our world through different eyes – and the view of God. It demands we deliberate on our predicaments. It puts the strange words of God in Christ into our mouths. We wait to see what is born and what we might speak. What that is, or what will be said, is open-ended and even disturbing. It is also ineluctable in its promise of God's doing a 'new thing' and making us a 'new creation' (Isa. 43.19; 2 Cor. 5.17).

We are called to live as if the kingdom of God or heaven is where we reside in the here-and-now. This sensibility, now nearly lost, was once commonplace in the early Christian tradition of the fourth and fifth centuries.

St Leo the Great preached that 'having confidence in such a great promise ... be citizens of heaven, not only in hope, but also in your daily life'.[11] Or, as we might express it nowadays, the earth is to be a 'thin place' where heaven breaks in and coincides with our lived reality. 'We belong to a different world,' Gregory of Nazianzus likewise wrote, 'far more sublime and abiding than the one you see around you.'[12] As we live as citizens of heaven, our lives on earth are transformed. We see our interconnectedness with one another and the moral demands that places upon us. 'Give bread and seize paradise',[13] admonished John Chrysostom as he enjoined charitable love as the cornerstone of Christian living.

Far from being an escapist or imaginary fantasy, the vision of hope contained within the kingdom of God or heaven was seen to require hard work, courage, fortitude and resilience. St Paul wrote that he '[pressed] on towards the goal for the prize of the heavenly calling of God in Christ Jesus' (Phil. 2.14). St Augustine of Hippo assured believers that 'the crown of victory is promised to those who engage in the struggle'.[14] God (and not human effort) would be the guarantor of history – but we would have to toil as God's purpose unfurls.

We live in an age in which we sorely need to retrieve 'heaven' as a vision of hope and a locus of action for our immediate present.

The evidence of potentially catastrophic climate change caused by human consumption and pollution is incontrovertible, even if cranks try to deny it. The overwhelming scientific data and proof do not need rehearsing or defending here. The news is filled year after year with rising seas, savage wildfires, murderous storms, chaotic temperatures, and the decline and death of natural habitats and species. The earth is plundered, abused and killed. The old world has burned in the fires of industry. The new world born is shaped by unbridled consumer capitalism. The scenes and headlines are apocalyptic in quality and tone. The world is ending unless people repent and change their ways. Justice demands our attention. The impact of the climate crisis does not fall evenly, even in human terms. The poorest, ethnic minority/global majority heritage peoples, women, and the disabled are the hardest hit and most vulnerable.

The prophets of our modern age are secular. They are ecologists and ecological activists, perhaps none so famous as Greta Thunberg. In 2019, she addressed the World Economic Forum at Davos saying: 'Our house is on fire. I am here to say, our house is on fire ... We are less than 12 years away from not being able to undo our mistakes.' Thunberg brushed away the soft paternalism offered to the youth of today:

Adults keep saying: *We owe it to the young people to give them hope.* But I don't want your hope. I don't want you to be hopeful. I want you to panic. I want you to feel the fear I feel every day. And then I want you to act. I want you to act as you would in a crisis. I want you to act as if the house was on fire.

While some may find the words of Thunberg (and others like her) alarmist, the apocalyptic mood reveals that we are living in a current state of crisis for humanity and the natural world. Denial or inaction are impossible. As in the book of Joel, God pours the Spirit out on all people at the end of the ages, and it is our 'sons and daughters' who prophesy (Joel 2.28).

The climate crisis has two sides that need to be addressed with urgency. On one side, there can be no doubt that there need to be profound and far-reaching changes in individual and collective human behaviours, both for the common good of humanity and for the whole created order. On the other side, there must be a wholesale re-evaluation of a world order built on continual economic growth through exploitation of the earth and the people of the earth.

This is where we can see 'heaven' as both partly the cause of the crisis and partly the solution.

In a famous essay published in 1967, the American historian Lynn White argued that the historical roots of the modern ecological crisis were in medieval Christianity. The advances in science and technology that we see as the hallmarks of the modern period began in the medieval period, whose view of humanity and nature was formed by the Judaeo-Christian tradition. This view placed human beings as the apex of the created order. The Bible, especially Genesis 1.28, was taken to give a divine mandate for humanity to 'have dominion over' and 'subdue' the earth. As White put it, in this worldview, 'man and nature are two things, and man is master'.[15] When this worldview was allied with technological and scientific development in the modern period, the western tendency to exploit the natural world was inexorable. It led to what White called Christianity's 'huge burden of guilt'.

White's argument has not been without its critics. Nevertheless, it has influenced many others to see Christianity as part of the crisis of climate change and the emergency we face.

We should be concerned about the theological legacy that shapes how we view our relationship to the world and how we act. Studies show that belief in an afterlife is associated with lower estimates of the risks posed by climate change. Conservative Christians are more likely to deny climate change than others in the population. While correlation does not equate with causation, it is not hard to see why belief in an otherworldly heaven contributes to climate change denial. This is especially true when it is allied with political cultures suspicious of worldly authorities and fond of conspiracy theories. In addition to apparent scriptural mandates to dominate and subdue the earth, apocalyptic texts such as Revelation 21.1 talk about the 'passing away' of this earth and God's dramatic creation of a 'new heaven and a new earth'. Indeed, the Bible seems to say that the present earth will be burned in fire as part of God's plan (2 Peter 3.7). Not only does the Bible appear to legitimate the mass exploitation of the earth, it seems to suggest that the consequences (even if admitted as real) do not matter. God will swoop in and make everything new in some future but otherworldly reality. The end times are coming. We should carry on as normal.

Heaven is part of the problem we face in our ecological crisis. We have rendered it impotent by placing it as separate from and discontinuous with this world, concerned with eternal consolation rather than immediate change.

Heaven can be part of the solution too, however, if we understand it rightly and capture it as part of a daily sacred art of contemplation. As we face a climate emergency, heaven offers a radical resource to shape how we view the world and our place within it, and how we ought to act.

As we have seen, Scripture speaks of 'heaven and earth' in one breath as one world where God dwells. In the first creation story of Genesis, God makes, sees and declares creation as good. God delights in it. God wills its flourishing as one world. God dwells there. The Lord's Prayer instructs that heaven and earth are called to coincide as part of the coming of God's kingdom. The kingdom of heaven spoken of in Matthew's Gospel is a present and future reality. In Christ, it has already broken in. In Christ, it will be completed. The kingdom of heaven circumscribes heaven and earth. It is near and among us. It orients us to be in Christ through whom all things in heaven and earth were made (John 1.3; Col. 1.16; Heb. 1.2; Rev. 3.14). It is a way of being that seeks right relations between people, the earth and God.

As Christ indwells us and we dwell in him through the Holy Spirit, we are connected to everything in heaven and earth. We live in intricate networks of dependence, primarily on God but also on the whole created order. Christ came to 'save sinners' (1 Tim. 1.15) but his saving work transforms all of creation (Eph. 1.10; Col. 1.19–20). Christ is a cosmic figure, rather than one simply concerned with human affairs. 'We know that the whole creation has been groaning as in the pains of childbirth right up to the present time,' wrote St Paul (Rom. 8.22). 'Being in Christ' refers us to consider our relationship to him, to his creation, and to his redemption of 'heaven and earth' as one world. 'Being in Christ' is the dynamic location of the kingdom of heaven. It gives us a vision of hope where we can see the future transforming our reality here-and-now.

Criticisms such as those we have seen in this chapter rightly chastise our sense of heaven. We must learn to read scriptural texts in a way attuned to 'being in Christ' as the hope of all creation. As we do, heaven unveils the sacred quality of the earth, our humbled place within creation, and our responsibility.

It shapes an apocalyptic imagination that, far from being disengaged from the world, sees heaven as embroiling us in the birth pangs of a renewed creation. Heaven means the openness of God to the world. It calls us to the struggle for ecological justice in the present. It calls us to share in God's making new all things in heaven and earth, with Christ at the heart.

Two examples of reading scriptural texts in such an ecological manner can be seen in how we read Genesis 1 and Revelation 21, the beginning and the end of the Bible, the first and the last creation stories.

Genesis 1 offers the first creation story. While human beings are afforded a unique status as made in the 'image' and 'likeness of God' (Gen. 1.26), they are not the apogee of creation as is often assumed. The pinnacle of creation is the Sabbath (Gen. 2.1–3). The Sabbath rest, rather than humankind, is the goal and crown of creation.

Human beings exist as one part of the ecological system of the 'heavens and the earth' created by God. They do not exist apart from it or over it as lords or masters. In Genesis, humanity is created alongside other animals. 'Adam' means 'of the earth', just as 'Eve' means 'daughter of life'. The heavens and the earth are made for what the eco-theologian Celia Deane-Drummond calls the 'active appreciation' of resting in God through the Sabbath.[16] This active appreciation means finding fulfilment in the sense of interconnectedness and intricate web of dependency on one another and God.

The call to 'have dominion' and 'subdue' the earth does not mean, then, that human beings are mandated to dominate or exploit it. Christian and Jewish scholars argue that Genesis 1.28 means we bear the image and likeness of God insofar as we care for and tend the natural world in which we live. For Christians, dominion is exercised after the pattern of Christ, who emptied himself and became servant of all (Phil. 2.7). Jesus is the image of God (Col. 1.15). Insofar as we have our being in Christ, we carry that image and likeness of God. We are to share in the reconciling work of Christ that touches upon all creation, subduing the injustices that mar it. Humanity is called to keep the earth as God keeps it, namely with care and love (Gen. 2.15).

The Sabbath which forms the pinnacle of creation calls us to practise humble awareness. In the Sabbath, 'heaven and earth' rest in God. In rest, we recognize our connection with and dependence upon the natural world, as well as our moral responsibility for it and one another. In the Sabbath, we see all of this as a wondrous and mysterious gift from God. The Sabbath denies that we can separate ourselves from creation and God. When we fail to observe the Sabbath, we isolate ourselves and subject creation to violence.

The contemplation envisaged in the Sabbath is not dispassionate or divorced from a call to action in the present. We must not fail to act on what we know is right. Seeing needs to lead to doing. As we contemplate nature, we 'begin to hear the "silent voice" of creation and its demands', as Deane-Drummond puts it.[17] The Sabbath generates a principle of resistance. As we see the integral value of creation and our humble place within it, we are called to resist ecological injustices, which include both the human damage done to the environment and natural habitats and the disproportionate impact of climate change on the most vulnerable in human societies.

Pope Francis' encyclical *Laudato Si'* issued in 2015 represents the most influential Christian publication on the environment that pulls together much of this kind of re-reading of what creation means. The encyclical was addressed to 'every living person on this planet' and concerns itself with 'care for our common home'.[18] It takes its title from Francis of Assisi's 'Canticle of the Creatures' and means 'praise be to you'. That meaning directs the reader to understand that environmental care involves attentive love for the earth and its peoples as an expression of joyful gratitude to God – the very character of the Sabbath.

For Pope Francis, we are called to an 'ecological conversion' by which an encounter with Jesus as our hope leads to deeper communion with God, neighbour and all of creation.[19] He calls this kind of communion an 'integral ecology', one which considers humanity's place within ecosystems. Within an 'integral ecology', we must consider the ethical and spiritual character of how we belong and interact with the natural world and the human inhabitants of the world. Environmental care intersects with social justice. As Pope Francis writes, 'strategies for a solution demand an integrated approach to combating poverty, restoring dignity to the excluded, and at the same time protecting nature'.[20]

This integral ecology places demands upon both communal and individual lives, from the global order all the way down to every one of us. *Laudato Si'* calls for international agreements to attend both to how we can protect the environment and to how we can order the world to the common good of all. On a more individual level, the encyclical calls for each one of us to attend to focusing less on consumerism, receiving environmental education, taking joy in our natural world, and joining in forms of love that issue in civic action. This is the kind of 'resistance' that issues from the character of keeping the Sabbath.

Having considered the significance of the first 'creation' story in Genesis 1, we can now look at the last 'creation' story. This will flesh out further an apocalyptic imagination that sees 'heaven' and 'earth' as one integral whole spanning an arc from creation to redemption. This apocalyptic imagination places ecological responsibilities upon us as we share in the work of God to love the earth and its peoples.

Revelation 21 offers the last creation story in the Bible. Or we rather might say 're-creation' story, for it looks to the end of the ages rather than the beginning. The book of Revelation was written during a period of Roman imperial persecution of Christians. This first-century crisis made the writer of Revelation look to the end for hope. Its dramatic visions of cataclysmic conflict between the forces of good and evil, divine judgement, and the return of Christ mark out Revelation as the only fully apocalyptic writing of the New Testament. It concludes with a vision of a 'new heaven and a new earth; for the first heaven and the first earth had passed away' (Rev. 21.1). In this new creation, a 'new Jerusalem' comes down from heaven (Rev. 21.9–21). The 'old' world becomes charged with the heavenly grandeur of God. God dwells no longer in a temple, but among the inhabitants of the city, providing its light (Rev. 21.22–24). The paradise lost in Genesis is restored (Rev. 22.1–7). In the new 'heaven and earth', God's presence radically reconfigures human community and the natural world into heavenly harmony for all time.

As we have seen, there are those who read the re-creation of the 'heavens and earth' and the 'passing away' of the old as meaning the annihilation of this world. That gives tacit licence either to disregard environmental degradation or to see environmental care as a nicety rather than as an urgent demand. After all, in the end, God will destroy this world and give us a new one. There is an otherworldly solution to ecological crisis.

This is, of course, a fundamentally mistaken and flawed interpretation. We have seen the intrinsic value of creation given in the Scriptures, the moral demand to care for the earth as a gift, and the call to exercise justice to the peoples of the earth. But this misreading of Revelation 21 is a dangerous possibility, and one that shapes some Christian attitudes.

The Ghanaian theologian John Ekem develops an alternative reading of Revelation 21, which he suggests represents a 'theology of hope' in our environmental crisis, just as it gave hope to the early persecuted Christian communities.[21] For Ekem, the book of Revelation gives a vision of the 'radical renewal of creation' rather than its inevitable destruction. His reading rejects any shortsighted view that ignores present-day concerns. He draws out how Revelation 21 offers hope for 'African communities in search of holistic salvation amidst the hydra-headed challenges confronting the continent', ranging from ecological calamity through to related poverty and inequality.[22]

Ekem's 'theology of hope' remains pertinent to all of us, presenting a different way of inhabiting the apocalyptic imagination of Revelation 21. It is worth unpacking in more detail.

For Ekem, readings sensitive to African cultures and perspectives call us to think beyond human-centred concerns. He quotes from another contemporary Ghanaian theologian, Joseph Mante, to illustrate the change in perspective and imagination required. Mante writes that an environmental theology suited to Africa must move away from a western 'mechanistic view of nature', 'insist on the relationality of every entity to its environment', and 'incorporate salvation history within an ecological framework'.[23]

Ekem's theology of hope draws upon African notions of time to reconsider how the 'future' is that which gives dynamic shape and force to the direction of the present in view of the past. The future gives an immediate vision of what might, can, or should be. Insofar as there is a sense of the future, it exists to inform action in the present to make that future real in the here-and-now. The future can disrupt the present status quo and work against the injustices of the past.

Ekem then applies this sense in which the future informs and shapes the here-and-now to Ghanaian translations of Revelation 21 into mother-tongue Asante-Twi and Gã languages.[24] In both instances, 'the prospects of a new heaven and a new earth' are viewed in both future and present senses simultaneously. What God promises breaks into the here-and-now. The Gã concept of 'newness', for example, means 'divinely breathed radical renewal'. Re-creation entails radical renewal rather than replacement. Likewise, the Asante-Twi concept of 'dwelling' (literally 'pitching a tent') used to translate the verses about God making his home among mortals (Rev. 21.4) implies that 'God himself will take the initiative to alleviate our sufferings'. This dwelling is not some otherworldly reality pushed off into an indefinite future. It remains relevant for current concerns about human survival and ecological balance.

We all can learn from Ekem's 'theology of hope'. It informs a proper apocalyptic imagination about 'heaven and earth' as one creation. This apocalyptic imagination shapes our ecological sensibility and sensitivity. Heaven is a dynamic reality of God's presence; the earth is already connected to heaven. It will be drawn into full communion with heaven at the end, and that end draws the present forward even now.

In this apocalyptic imagination, salvation pertains to the entirety of 'heaven and earth', rather than just humanity. 'In hope', wrote St Paul, '... the creation itself will be set free from its bondage to decay and will obtain the freedom of the glory of the children of God' (Rom. 8.20–1). God's will 'set forth in Christ' is a 'plan for the fullness of time, to gather up all things in him, things in heaven and things on earth' (Eph. 1.10). As we attend to the end of the earth and heaven, we see that God holds the past, present and future together in mutual interdependence.

Heaven matters, then, as an immediate reality. It probably looks different from what most of us imagine at first when we think of the word. It demands our immediate attention. It unveils the loving presence of God in creation. It lingers as the promise of fulfilment, already here and yet also to come.

Heaven both instructs and chastens us in relation to our ecological crisis. Heaven demands searching for the ways of God. It transforms who we think we are, what the world is, how we relate to it, and how we should act. We share in and cooperate with the coming of the kingdom of heaven.

On the one hand, we must learn as Christian communities how to bring the best out from our old traditions. We must attend to the movement of God in history as witnessed to in the Scriptures and in our practices of faith. Prayer, keeping the Sabbath, worship, a biblical sense of the integral goodness of the world, and the spiritual sight of God's presence in the one world of 'heaven and earth' – these are all principles of resistance against environmental injustice against the earth and its peoples.

Likewise, we must remain open to new treasures, whether from within our communities or from the wisdom and insight of scientists, children, other people of faith, and ecological activists. We must seek points of solidarity in the pursuit of justice.

Drawing upon old and new treasures enables our sharing in the coming of the kingdom of heaven. Environmental crisis demands we respond together urgently as we look for this coming. Like the crowds who followed Jesus, we must 'take the kingdom of heaven by force' – which means with relentless passion as fierce as violence. We are called to be caught up into God's saving work, along with the whole of creation.

On the other hand, we must also learn to live in messy complexity. We must identify the ways in which we, our communities and religious traditions cultivate and bear sin against the earth and peoples of the earth. We must remain open, then, to God's disruptive activity that unveils our complicity in sinful attitudes and structures. We have seen the ways in which Christianity has at times taken heaven to mean something that ends up destroying rather than building up justice in relation to the earth and the peoples of the earth. We need to repent of the ways in which our imaginations and actions have led to a very different and troubling form of violently storming the kingdom of heaven. By violently pushing heaven off into some indeterminate future, we have stolen its radical potential for hope and change in the present world.

The kingdom of heaven, insofar as it exists, comes as a gift from God. It does not emerge from broken human communities in any manner evacuated of God's influence or love. If we think it does – and we often have – we unavoidably replicate human structures of violent inequality and injustice, so that the earth ends up more closely resembling hell than heaven. If we do not search ourselves and our traditions, we fail to pray and live out 'your will be done, on earth as it is in heaven'. As we long for an end to injustice of all forms, we must search to know why the existing order of things endures – and how we contribute to that.

At the end, heaven reminds us that God has radical priority in the marriage of heaven and earth, as creator and as redeemer. If we think ourselves capable of saving the earth on our own, we will lose sight of our brokenness and need for God. We will view ourselves as 'masters' of salvation, ill attuned to the ways in which our faith and wider society remain complicit in sins against the earth and peoples of the earth. We will assume, as western modernity has, that we can perfect this world through human technology. Like modernity, we will fail to look for the disruptive activity of God in every nook and cranny of our lives together. Our apocalyptic imagination will fail to be as radical as it might be. The world as we know it needs to end – including our individual worlds and the world of the Church. Rather than just technological advance, we need entirely new ways of relating to the earth and its peoples.

We need heaven in the here-and-now to suffuse our apocalyptic imagination. We need the God of heaven to lead and light our way as we are drawn to the marriage of heaven and earth. Then our promised future will be our present. In God, everything scattered that was, is, and is yet to come remains, as the poet Dante put it, 'bound by love into one single volume'.

Notes

1 Dante Alighieri, *The Divine Comedy*, trans. Allen Mandelbaum, New York, London, Toronto: Everyman's Library, 1995, p. 539.

2 Karl Marx, 'A Contribution to the Critique of Hegel's Philosophy of Right: Introduction' in J. J. O'Malley (ed.), *Marx: Early Political Writings*, Cambridge: Cambridge University Press, 1994, p. 57.

3 Marx, 'A Contribution to the Critique of Hegel's Philosophy of Right', p. 58.

4 Paula Gooder, *Heaven*, London: SPCK, 2011, p. xii.

5 Basil of Caesarea, *Letters*, 8, in Edward Condon (ed.), *Death, Judgement, Heaven & Hell*, Washington, DC: The Catholic University of America Press, 2019, p. 70.

6 Theodoret of Cyrus, *Commentary on the Psalms*, 87.5, in Condon (ed.), *Death, Judgement, Heaven & Hell*, p. 70.

7 Leo the Great, *Sermons*, 95.5, in Condon (ed.), *Death, Judgement, Heaven & Hell*, p. 68.

8 Elizabeth Conde-Frazier, *Atando Cabos: Latinx Contributions to Theological Education*, Grand Rapids, MI: Eerdmans, 2021, p. 39, quoting Padilla DeBorst.

9 Ada María Isasi-Diaz, 'Defining our "Proyecto Histórico": "Mujerista" Strategies for Liberation', *Journal of Feminist Studies in Religion*, vol. 9, nos 1–2 (1993), pp. 17–28.

10 Isasi-Diaz, 'Defining our "Proyecto Histórico"', p. 17.

11 Leo the Great, *Sermons*, 4, in Condon (ed.), *Death, Judgement, Heaven & Hell*, p. 52.

12 Gregory of Nazianzus, *Selected Orations*, 15.5, in Condon (ed.), *Death, Judgement, Heaven & Hell*, p. 53.

13 John Chrysostom, *On Repentance and Almsgiving*, 3.8, in Condon (ed.), *Death, Judgement, Heaven & Hell*, p. 63.

14 Augustine of Hippo, *The Christian Combat*, 1.1, in Condon (ed.), *Death, Judgement, Heaven & Hell*, p. 60.

15 Lynn White, 'The Historical Roots of Our Ecologic Crisis', *Science*, 155 (1967), pp. 1203–7.

16 Celia Deane-Drummond, *A Primer in Ecotheology: Theology for a Fragile Earth*, Eugene, OR: Cascade, 2017, p. 29.

17 Deane-Drummond, *A Primer in Ecotheology*, p. 30.

18 Pope Francis, *Laudato Si': On Care for Our Common Home*, Huntington, IN: Our Sunday Visitor, 2015, sect. 3.

19 Francis, *Laudato Si'*, sects 216–21.

20 Francis, *Laudato Si'*, sect. 139.

21 John D. K. Ekem, 'Revelation 21:1–4 from an African Perspective' in Gene L. Green, Stephen T. Pardue and K. K. Yeo (eds), *All Things New: Eschatology in the Majority World*, Carlisle: Langham, 2019, pp. 51–69.

22 Ekem, 'Revelation 21:1–4', p. 68.

23 Ekem, 'Revelation 21:1–4', p. 67.

24 Ekem, 'Revelation 21:1–4', pp. 62–5.

2

Hell

'Do not fear those who kill the body but cannot kill the soul;
rather fear him who can destroy both soul and body in hell.'
(Matthew 10.28)

Abandon every hope, who enter here.
(Dante Alighieri, *Inferno*, 3.9)[1]

Hell is other people.
(Jean-Paul Sartre)

At first glance, the prospects around retrieving 'hell' as part of
the sacred art of contemplating the four last things seem bleak.
   Polls in the United Kingdom indicate that only around a
quarter of the British public believe in hell. Curiously, belief
in hell is nevertheless more popular in younger than older
generations, even if they are less inclined to believe in God. The
reasons for this are unknown. We might note, however, at least
a correlation with the drive for social justice that also marks
younger generations, keen to denounce injustice and inequality.
Likewise, in the USA fewer people believe in hell than heaven.
Of the roughly 60 per cent of Americans who believe in hell,
30 per cent consider it a place of eternal torment, while 40
per cent conceive of it as eternal separation from God. Insofar
as belief in hell persists, then, it is partial and fragmented.
   In the last chapter, we saw how the idea of heaven has faced
critical pressure. Hell faces an even deeper set of moral problems
related to how it has been traditionally conceived and depicted.
   Christian literature and art are replete with graphic accounts
of the horrors of hell which to modern sensibilities seem

barbaric. Dante's medieval epic poem *Inferno* laid out, for example, a complex geography of the circles of hell. In each circle, different sinners faced grotesque punishments that fitted their earthly sins. John Milton's early modern epic poem *Paradise Lost* alternatively portrayed hell as a prison from which the fallen angels plot the ruin and destruction of God's creation as an act of revenge upon the 'God of heaven'. Medieval and early modern artists such as Jan van Eyck, Hieronymous Bosch and Michelangelo gleefully depicted hellscapes replete with demons, fires, torture and torments. Such images often formed altarpieces or adorned church walls. By striking fear into those who worshipped there, they encouraged obedience to the teachings of the Church, all upon pain of damnation.

Hell was not a minority concern in the Christian tradition. These various images of horror sprang out of mainstream Christian theology and preaching. Jesus seemed to call believers to fear the God who could 'destroy both body and soul in hell' (Matt. 10.28). The second-century *Apocalypse of Peter* morbidly depicted the fate of the damned at great length. The early Church Father and saint John Chrysostom wrote that 'in our churches we hear countless discourses on eternal punishment, on the rivers of fire, on the venomous worm, on bonds that cannot be burst, on exterior darkness'.[2] Other Christians had vivid visions of hell that they shared with others. Paschasius of Dumium in the sixth century, for example, wrote that he beheld 'an immeasurable sea of boiling fire, and men weeping and wailing', before throwing himself to the ground and praying 'that I may never endure the trials which are their fate'.[3] As the centuries passed, it became broadly agreed that the eternal terrors of hell expressed God's justice. The vision of hell instructed people through fear that they ought to mend their ways while they could. In modern evangelical parlance, the message was: turn or burn.

By the eleventh century, tales about infernal torments started to become the mainstay of parish sermons. Teachers and Christian theologians saw the utility of hell to provoke fear, which was useful as a means of correction and control. Writings and sermons gave lessons in horror. Honorius of Autun, for example, laid out in the twelfth century nine vivid torments that sinners should expect in hell. Manuals on Christian teaching translated these torments into tools for preachers. Through sermons, hell quickly permeated the minds and imaginations of ordinary Christians. The fear of hell promoted personal responsibility for one's actions and the possibility of changing one's ways before it was too late. It also cultivated obedience to the Church.

By the eighteenth century, the American Reformed theologian Jonathan Edwards was not unusual when he described how the redeemed would 'rejoice' as they gaze upon the punishments meted out upon the damned in hell. The source of joy for the blessed would be seeing 'the smoke of their torment and the raging of the flames of their burning' and hearing 'their dolorous shrieks and cries'.[4] Even as late as the nineteenth century, some Christians continued to preach 'hellfire' to induce fear and promote good behaviour. The Catholic priest John Furniss, for example, produced a pamphlet for children about 'the sight of hell' which detailed the fires, darkness, cacophony and putrid smell of the infernal realm, as well as 'the terrible face of the devil' as he gave out 'the tremendous sentence on the [damned] soul'.[5]

That the fear of hell was a repressive psychological tool full of violent imagery made it inherently suspicious to modern ears. Some Christians began to question the place of hell in the Christian imagination as a result. The British Prime Minister and Christian philosopher William Gladstone consigned the doctrine 'to sleep in a deep shadow as a thing needless in our enlightened and progressive age'.[6] The nineteenth-century author Lionel Tollemache likewise wrote that 'the wisest among us are seeking to drop Hell out of the Bible'.[7]

While some modern thinkers challenged the traditional inheritance of hell, it has nevertheless persisted in many Christian communities. This persistence troubles many people. Contemporary New Atheists decry the psychological damage caused by teaching belief in hell as akin to child abuse, such is the trauma it still induces. Beyond that moral objection, it is hard – if not impossible – for most people to see how hell can be compatible with the simple biblical statement that 'God is Love' (1 John 4.7). Hell has become unpalatable and unviable to most modern sensibilities.

We ought to be sympathetic to the modern suspicions of the traditional notion of hell. The medieval poet Dante wrote that inscribed over the gates of hell were the words 'Abandon every hope, who enter here'. If the sacred art of contemplating the last things contains any vision of hope, it seems as if we would be better off leaving hell behind as a relic of the past. It seems as if we can't fathom how the 'primal love' of 'divine power' could ever be said to have made hell, as Dante also claimed.

Much like heaven, however, most people would be surprised to find that the Bible has a different concept of hell from the one we take for granted, and that the early Christian tradition also conceived of hell in different ways from what later became the dominant tradition with which we are more familiar.

What hell might mean, then, remains worth retrieving. We need to unpack what the Scriptures say. We also need to listen to voices of hope from the early Christian tradition. Like heaven, then, hell might still prove a helpful spiritual resource in two regards.

First, a re-formed sense of hell as self-induced can help us discern the work of God in the world here-and-now. Hell indeed does involve the absence of hope. Diagnosing what leads to that absence helps us see how we can join in with God's breaking into – and dismantling of – hell through Christ today. The diagnosis entails looking for the remedy of hope.

Second, as we retrieve a different sense of hell, we can see how restoring a sacred art of contemplating the last things such as hell speaks into modern crises. Seeing the hells of our own making unveiled also reveals from where our hope might come. As a case example, we can see how hell speaks into the re-emergence of populist politics in our contemporary world.

Let's begin by retrieving what the Scriptures say about hell.

Unlike 'the heavens and the earth', hell does not feature in any creation story in the Scriptures. Neither does hell appear in the Hebrew Scriptures at all. In other words, there is no concept of hell or an eternal place of punishment. In his 1971 song 'Imagine', John Lennon called listeners to picture a world in which there is 'no hell below us'. That was precisely the world, however, in which the Hebrew Scriptures emerged.

In the Hebrew Scriptures, all dead people went to *Sheol*. The word appears 63 times. Sometimes *Sheol* simply refers to a grave or a pit for the dead. At other times, it takes on a shadowy existence in the lower realms of the earth, although whether the descriptions are literal or metaphorical is disputed. Either way, in *Sheol* there are no feelings, memories, thoughts, light, sound, or praise of God (e.g. Eccl. 9.6, 10; Job 10.21-2;). Those in *Sheol* are shades who are trapped there (Job 10.21; Isa. 38.10). *Sheol* has an inexhaustible appetite and no limits (Prov. 1.12; Isa. 5.14). It is the deathly abode of the righteous and unrighteous alike. Some thought the dead were cut off from God in *Sheol* (Ps. 88.3-5; Isa. 38.11). Others believed that God's presence reached even to its dark depths and that God could deliver people from its grip (Ps. 139.8; 49.15).

Whether a literal place or not, *Sheol* was a bleak condition. In the Hebraic imagination, it only really mattered insofar as life is to be lived as fully and for as long as possible before inevitable death. Ideas of an afterlife in the Hebrew Scriptures predominantly referred not to the persistence of individual life but to the nation. The birth, life, death and revival of Israel were the abiding concerns of the prophets. The vision of the valley of dry bones in Ezekiel 37 is a good example. Later Christians often read this vision through the lens of the resurrection of the dead, seeing verses such as the breathing of new life into the skeletal remains as a vision of individual revival promised by Christ. That is mistaken. Ezekiel is clear that 'these bones are the whole house of Israel' (Ezek. 37.11).

We see developments by the time of the New Testament, whose writers used the language of *Sheol*, *Hades* and *Gehenna*. While translations sometimes render these words as 'hell', that is often misleading. The translation of these three words as hell elides their differences. It also injects far later images of what that word conjures.

In the New Testament, *Sheol* and *Hades* were conflated, joining the Hebraic idea of a shadowy house of the dead with Greek ideas about where people go when they die. The Hebraic idea of *Sheol* underwent some change as a result.

In Greek thought, *Hades* was a distinct underworld realm where the dead go. As the Greek idea developed, ideas also emerged about *Hades* including a place of judgement for the wicked called *Tartarus*.

The early Christians began to repurpose *Sheol* in relation to the Greek ideas of *Hades* and *Tartarus*. In the Christian Scriptures, *Hades* was closely associated with death, often in personified forms (e.g. Rev. 1.18; 6.8). Sometimes *Hades* was imagined to be a temporary condition of death from which God will rescue someone, especially the Chosen One or Messiah (e.g. Acts 2.27, 32). At other times, *Hades* was a place of torment for the wicked (e.g. Luke 16.23). The sense that God punished the sinner only began to emerge towards the end of the Hebrew scriptural period (for example, Dan. 12.1–3) and grew in Jewish thought in the two centuries before Christ's first coming. There was also the sense in the New Testament that *Hades* was a principle opposed to heaven but which has no substantial power over God or those who follow Christ (e.g. Matt. 16.18).

It is the language of *Gehenna*, however, that brings us closest to our stereotypical ideas of hell.

Gehenna occurs 12 times across the Gospels of Matthew, Mark and Luke, as well as in the Epistle of James. *Gehenna* is often translated as 'hell', but it actually means the 'valley of Hinnom'. The Hebrew Scriptures recorded that *Gehenna* was originally a valley south-west of Jerusalem where children were burned as sacrifices to the Ammonite god Moloch (2 Chron. 28.3; 2 Kings 16.3; 21.6; Jer. 32.35). As part of the religious reform and revival under Josiah, *Gehenna* was cleared of such abominable practices (2 Kings 23.1–25). Josiah left it as a desecrated place. It became a byword for God's judgement against apostasy (Jer. 7.29–34; 19.1–15; Isa. 66.24). It also became seen as a possible place of redemption where a 'valley of dead bodies and ashes' would become 'sacred to the Lord' (Jer. 31.40). Where judgement was envisaged, annihilation rather than eternal torment was the punishment. It also could still be a site of salvation.

In the New Testament, *Gehenna* was pictured in stark terms. It is not clear that it was seen as a place of future eternal destruction, however, rather than what might happen in the present. At the time, *Gehenna* remained an 'accursed place' (1 Enoch 27.1). It was seen as a place of spiritual death suited only for the unrighteous. Jesus taught that it was better to strike off part of the body that caused sin than to enter whole into that terrible place of fire (Mark 9.43–48; Matt. 5.22, 29–30; 18.9). Jesus warned his followers to fear God who could cast them into *Gehenna* (Luke 12.4–5; Matt. 10.28). Hypocrites and those who opposed the kingdom of God belonged there (Matt. 23.33). The Epistle of James described how false teaching that cursed 'those who are made in the likeness of God' shared in the fires of *Gehenna* (James 3.6). *Gehenna* was abominable. Yet it was a real and present place that carried a deep power of spiritual meaning.

Closely related to *Gehenna* in the New Testament were the ideas of an 'eternal fire' or 'lake of fire'. These ideas were later taken up with glee and developed into the notion of hell as an imagined and otherworldly destination for the damned. These are the images with which we have become familiar over the centuries. It is not clear, however, that this is what the scriptural references intended. Matthew 25.41–46, for example, imagined the judgement of the nations at the end of time 'when the Son of Man comes in his glory'. In Matthew's account, those who have failed to treat those in need as if they were Christ would be 'accursed'. Christ will command them to 'depart from me into the eternal fire prepared for the devil and his angels'. Likewise, Revelation pictured a 'lake of fire' four times, as a place or condition at the end of the ages into which God would cast the 'beast' and 'false prophets' (19.20), the devil (20.10), death and *Hades* (20.14–15), and the morally reprobate (21.8). Such fire destroys all that has opposed God and the kingdom of heaven. 'Fire' seems to function again as a metaphor for divine rejection, however, rather than as a literal and perpetual punishment. Annihilation rather than torment was in view.

Three things are clear, then.

First, there was no final, determinative, or fully formed concept of hell in the Scriptures that directly maps on to the later notions of hell that emerged. Rather, there are a range of distinct (if overlapping) evocative images. Most commonly these images attempt to describe a condition of mortality or of moral standing that prevents communion with God. Exclusion from God's presence was terrible. Being excluded from the kingdom of God was imaged in parables as being cast into 'darkness' where there would be 'weeping and gnashing of teeth' (e.g. Matt. 8.12; Luke 13.28). Exclusion was seen, however, as a psychological condition of deep dismay and pained anguish rather than as a place of perpetual physical penalty.

Second, the real emphasis in the New Testament was on hope rather than hell. The key message revolved around how 'God was in Christ reconciling the world to himself' (2 Cor. 5.19). This reconciliation included the idea of Jesus visiting the 'spirits in prison' (1 Pet. 3.18–22). Some early Christians developed this into the notion of Christ's descent into hell to deliver humanity from captivity to sin and death. In western Christianity, the Apostles' Creed, composed around the fifth century, declared as a basic belief that Christ 'descended into hell' between his death and resurrection. The Old English name for this was the 'harrowing of hell', meaning 'the despoiling'. In eastern Christianity, icons often depicted the resurrection by showing the doors of hell broken open with Christ pulling up Adam and Eve (the parents of humankind) into new life. Hell was overcome. Liberation was promised and secured by Christ.

Third, later elaborate views of hell as a place of eternal punishment can, nevertheless, trace some of their origins to the scriptural images. That these in any way directly represent what Jesus intended remains, however, doubtful.

There is an alternative.

Hell represents 'this-worldly' aspects of reality. It describes an atrophied spiritual condition of alienation from God and one another insofar as we are made in God's image. Hell is the crisis of communion. In this sense, retrieving the credibility of hell remains morally vital. It allows us to diagnose what leads to such crisis. Having the reality of hell unveiled to us remains crucial in how we can work with the hopeful grain of God's love to dismantle and escape it. In this sense, hell is a vital part of developing an apocalyptic imagination which enfolds us into the hope constituted by the dynamic saving work of God.

We can now turn to what this apocalyptic imagination about hell looks like.

The scholar of religion David Bentley Hart rejects the 'spiritual squalor of the traditional concept of an eternal hell'.[8] He turns to the early tradition of Christian 'universalists' to offer an alternative vision of hope. These are Christians who 'believe that in the end all persons will be saved and joined to God in Christ'.[9] Universalists drew upon scriptural warrants for universal salvation or *apokatastasis*. In John 12.32, Jesus spoke of how at the end of time he would 'draw all people to myself'. St Paul wrote in Ephesians 1.9–10 about God's 'plan for the fullness of time' to gather up in Christ 'all things in heaven and on earth'. Acts 3.21 likewise describes a 'universal restoration' (*apokatastasis*) of all of creation.

Hart charts how such universalism was a highly popular view in the first 500 years of Christianity. It was so widespread that universalists became known as *misericordes*, meaning 'the merciful hearted'.

These 'merciful hearted' believed in hell but not in its eternity. Early theologians such as Clement of Alexandria, Origen and Gregory of Nyssa thought of hell as a remedial place of purification before final union with God. In the fourth century, for example, Diodorus of Tarsus wrote that the wicked were to be 'purified for a brief period according to the amount of malice in their works ... but immortal blessedness having no end awaits them.'[10]

For many of the universalists, that hell was not for ever

hinged upon the right translation of the Greek word *aeon*. While the Latin word for 'eternal' became an accepted translation of *aeon*, universalists argued that the Greek referred to a 'long but limited period of time'. This is the common meaning of the word in its anglicized form, where an 'aeon' means 'an age' or 'a period'. If we accept the claim of the universalists, then 'eternal hell' would be better understood as 'hell for a discrete period of time appointed by God as part of the plan of salvation'. Such a vision of hope seemed to accord better with notions of divine justice proportionate to sins committed. The mercy of divine love conditions divine justice, rather than vice versa.

These merciful hearted universalists believed that all creation and all humanity would ultimately be restored to an original state of bliss through the loving mercy of God. The seventh-century St Isaac the Syrian asserted, for example, that God's love was 'timeless and everlasting' and was 'spread out over all creation'. In that divine love, nothing 'will be lost, as far as God is concerned' in the heavenly kingdom of God. 'Not even the immense wickedness of the demons', concluded Isaac, 'can overcome the measure of God's goodness.'[11]

The *misericordes* faded into a minority opinion in later centuries, largely thanks to the dominance of St Augustine of Hippo's thought in Christian theology from the fifth century onwards. Augustine taught the idea of an 'eternal hell' and its fittingness in relation to divine justice. 'You confess the torment,' wrote Augustine, 'then confess that it is deserved'.[12] 'Surely,' he wrote elsewhere, 'just as sin is unjust, the punishment for sin is just.'[13] As Augustine's influence on Christian thought cemented, his opinion became the majority view. As already noted, this majority view filtered through to the pews of ordinary Christians in the medieval practices of contemplating the horrors of hell as a call to moral reform and obedience. This view became what we now often assume hell has always meant.

What was once a majority view, however, does not need to continue to be so.

Although Roman Catholicism has largely maintained the traditional teachings about hell, others have listened to the moral and logical reservations about them. The past century has seen various ecumenical attempts to retrieve universalism, including that of David Bentley Hart in the Orthodox tradition. Universalists have tried to rescue the moral and intellectual credibility of hell. They disambiguate later theological opinion from what the Scriptures say. They suggest it is more coherent and palatable to see how God's love conditions divine justice rather than vice versa. As John Robinson put it, 'in a universe of love there can be no heaven which tolerates a chamber of horrors'.[14] They also read the complex arc of scriptural texts within the basic and hopeful principle that God's saving will is to 'reconcile all things to himself' (Col. 1.19).

In the end, universalists and those sympathetic to universalism promote the hope that love conquers all. Love renders even hell obsolete in the triumph of grace. If hell exists, then God's love means that we have hope to believe that it will be an empty place at the end of the ages.

Theological attempts to reread the meaning of hell have been more than matched by its persistence in wider and popular modern thought. Pre-modern belief in an eternal underworld has diminished along with religious conviction. Yet the idea of hell has endured as a powerful description of sorrow and strife in this life. The hellscapes of modernity are theatres of war, genocides, environmental degradation, systemic racism and exploitative economies, to name but a few. These self-induced variations of 'hell on earth' still erupt in new ways into the fabric of our daily lives now.

The tendency to use hell to describe this-worldly realities has depth to it from which we can also learn. It represents more than shallow lip-service to the idea of hell. The American sociologist Peter Berger described the persistence of hell as a 'signal of transcendence' still to be found in the modern world.[15] Hell provides a language that describes the tragic reality of broken human relations, diagnosing the cause of those realities and bearing moral judgement upon them. Only hell allows us to articulate and engage with the reprehensibility of insidious forms of human brokenness. It allows us to envisage a radically different future, just as much as heaven does.

If we are to retrieve hell as part of restoring the sacred art of contemplating the last things, then we have much to learn. We ought to attend to both the merciful hearted universalists and the modern tendency that links hell to the here-and-now.

This retains the moral urgency of hell rather than pushing it off into an indefinite future or otherworldly realm. It focuses on the human character and causation of hell. Hell becomes a social reality opposed to the kingdom of heaven. Hell becomes a diagnosis of this-worldly ills. If 'hell is empty', then 'all the devils are here', to quote from William Shakespeare's *The Tempest*. Unveiling the this-worldly nature of hell means we are called to reform our ways now. This moral reformation is not to ward off punishment in some indefinite future. It is to join in with the coming of God in Christ now and the liberation it brings. It is to retain hope that hell is neither inevitable nor final.

We are in dire need of such hope.

The divisive spectre of populism haunts the world. It feeds on hell and creates hell. Populism derives from a Latin root meaning 'the people'; they claim to give voice to the people. Populists are mad as hell about something on behalf of the people. Populism refers, then, to a certain form of politics that opposes the will of the people to some perceived corrupt elite or other. 'Us' becomes pitted against 'them' in a world perceived to have run amok. Us often means a particular ethnic, religious or national identity. Populists want to send the them to hell. Sometimes the them are the governing or economic elites. At other times, the them are ethnic and religious minorities, immigrants, feminists or LGBTQ+ peoples. While populism can spark healthy debate, it often spills over into violence and hate crimes. When it does, it creates living hells for vulnerable peoples.

Populism emerges in times of social upheaval and crisis, many of which recent decades have seen in abundance. Hyper-globalization, mass migration, automation, corruption, and increases in poverty are the typical kinds of factor that have led to social upheaval and crisis.

Populists are disenchanted. They feel powerless. Populism blames the them for where we find ourselves. It calls for radical change, typically back to some supposed golden age free from the influence of the them. Populism is often spearheaded by a charismatic leader. These leaders style themselves as the 'voice of the people' against the 'them'. Populist leaders and groups have surged in status across the world, especially in Europe and the Americas. Some have even been elected to the highest political offices with immense geopolitical reach.

While populism identifies real social tensions, it can also cynically exploit them and deepen division. Populist groups occur across the political spectrum but often sit uneasily with the values of a liberal democracy, especially the commitment to pluralism. At its extreme, populism threatens the democratic process itself. It typically undermines the free press, judiciary and governmental checks and balances that underpin stable and fair governance. It feeds on misinformation and conspiracy theories. It erodes the freedom of citizens. It stokes up hatred and lets it seep in deep. Once in power, populist leaders typically cling on. Constitutional norms are bulldozed over. Stable democracy and a plural society where difference is protected all become eroded. The kind of liberal democracy once thought to be the fulfilment of history has now become an endangered species.

What is not often noted, however, is that populism has a spiritual character. Daniel Nilsson DeHanas, a contemporary scholar, argues that 'populism is a spiritual style of doing politics' in three ways.[16]

First, the 'us' versus 'them' narrative sets 'sacred boundaries' in place between the 'pure' and 'impure'. Populists use battle cries about protecting borders or preventing cultural invasions to keep 'us' safe. These boundaries between us and them are inviolable. They even justify violence and the spreading of lies against the dangerous and impure them to protect the sacred us.

Second, charismatic leaders of populist movements are often attributed with 'supernatural' energy and perceived to have supernatural attributes not possessed by many. In prosaic terms, we can see how populist leaders often style themselves as geniuses, uniquely and solely capable of reversing some perceived negative situation. A cult of personality forms around these supernaturally charismatic leaders, representing the 'will of the people' and adamantly opposing the 'them' or 'other'.

Third, populist movements and their leaders are often apocalyptic in a negative sense. Populist leaders carry dark visions of the world under apocalyptic peril. At times, they even cast themselves as the fulfilment of apocalyptic prophecies from the Jewish, Christian and Islamic traditions. In dystopian times, they say, their solutions alone will save and restore society. Failure to listen will bring judgement and inevitable ruin. If people do not agree with them, then society can 'go to hell', and the populists will make sure it does.

What unites these three spiritual features of populism is an underlying spiritual sense of self-induced social alienation. We live in an alienated world. Hell as a condition speaks into that world. Understanding what constitutes this spiritual sense of hell will help diagnose what creates it. It will also lead to how we might dismantle hell with the triumph of grace.

We can see this sense of alienation as the hallmark of hell in two different fictional works of the twentieth century. The first is from the Christian apologist and writer C. S. Lewis; the second from the French philosopher and playwright Jean-Paul Sartre. These two fictional works diagnose what the condition of hell looks like in human terms.

In *The Great Divorce* first published in 1945, C. S. Lewis develops the narrator's journey from a place suggestive of hell to a vision of heaven. Hell is a banal, grey place of interminable boredom and mutually imposed isolation. Its residents are shadowy, insubstantial figures caught up in self-deceit. They are offered the opportunity of a visit to heaven, which some choose to take while others do not. Even some of those who travel to heaven nevertheless prefer to return to their hell. Towards the end of the narrator's journey, it is clear that 'the Gates of Hell are locked from the inside'. Human choices result in alienation from one another and from communion with the 'God of heaven'.

In *No Exit*, first performed in 1944, Jean-Paul Sartre's play depicts the afterlife where three damned souls are punished by being locked in a room together for eternity. None of them will take responsibility for causing their own damnation. They torment one another. They try to kill one another. They try to escape but cannot. Towards the end of the play, one character declares that 'hell is other people'.

While Lewis and Sartre picture these human-made hells differently, they share the sense that the real terror emanates from their inhumanity. Hell is a spiritual condition that misshapes human relationships and closes them off from one another – and from God.

They are not, however, pictures without hope. The 'spiritual guide' in Lewis's novel assures the narrator that heaven remains open to all who desire it. Sartre commented that the phrase 'hell is other people' is often misunderstood as meaning that 'our relations with other people are always poisoned, that they are invariably hellish relations'. What Sartre intended, however, was that 'if relations with someone else are twisted, vitiated, then that other person can only be hell'.[17] In other words, there is no fate but that which we choose.

What fictional works like those of Lewis and Sartre show us is that alienation is the root cause and defining feature of hell. As such, we can understand hell as a condition rather than as an underworld allotted for eternal punishment. Alienation describes the lack of human connection with other people or groups. It cascades into suspicion of the 'other', atrophying trust and dividing 'us' from 'them'. That is the hallmark of populism. Alienation blinds any sense of shared humanity. Unchecked, alienation issues in anger leading to exclusion and violence. The other becomes an object of scorn, vilified and humiliated. A hellish world emerges. Hell springs into being as a lived, broken and messy reality. We are imprisoned in a hell of our own making. Alienation kills hope. We may well indeed 'abandon every hope' as we enter hell. This is the broken world which populism grows. This is the world in which we find ourselves trapped.

Hope calls us to see the human cause and condition of such human-induced hell.

Hope unveils that what we should fear is not God. Rather we should fear those who 'can kill both body and soul', meaning the entirety of what it means to be known, seen and loved as fully human. Hope diagnoses the cause of hell as spiritual alienation. We see this in the case of populism, which seeks to colonize the mind by making us fail to see the 'other' as made in God's image. Rather, populists cast the 'them' as impure, as less than human, as worthy of being cast into hell. The currency of populism is humiliation of the 'other'.

Hope also provides a vision of dismantling the hell we make or in which we find ourselves cast. Hope calls us to begin with humility, not humiliation. We have to open ourselves back up to one another. That is risky. It leaves us vulnerable. But it is the start of joining in with God's making of all things new.

We can start dismantling hell by thinking again about where we locate hell and where we stand in relation to it.

Traditional theology has talked about hell as the 'kingdom of Satan'. This demonic kingdom is cast primarily as a place of post-mortem punishment. We might better talk about what the American Baptist theologian Walter Rauschenbusch called the 'Kingdom of Evil'. This Kingdom of Evil is firmly a human rather than a supernatural reality, while retaining a spiritual character. It is something to oppose as 'citizens of heaven', while also recognizing our sometimes-hidden complicity with it.

Rauschenbusch's ideas about the Kingdom of Evil emerged from within his lived experience of ministry in late nineteenth-century New York. He served on the edge of what was known as 'Hell's Kitchen', a neighbourhood notorious for poverty and crime. In this hell, Rauschenbusch advocated for what he called a 'Social Gospel'. The Social Gospel movement applied Christian teachings to social justice issues, seeing the 'good news' of Jesus Christ as the salvation not simply of individuals but of whole human societies. 'The Kingdom of God', wrote

Rauschenbusch, 'is humanity organized according to the will of God' and 'a progressive reign of love in human affairs'.[18] In other words, human beings were responsible for working with the grain of God's saving work to transform the broken societies in which they lived.

By contrast, the Kingdom of Evil emerged not from supernatural forces but from human origins. 'Theology with remarkable unanimity', Rauschenbusch declared, 'has discerned that sin is essentially selfishness' – and such selfishness marks fallen human societies.[19] 'Sin is transmitted', he wrote, 'along the lines of social tradition' and 'is absorbed by the individual from his social group'.[20] Collective sins appear as 'the super-personal forces of evil' which constitute the 'Kingdom of Evil' opposed to the 'Kingdom of God'.[21]

For Rauschenbusch, civic, political and economic institutions were the 'super-personal forces' or 'composite personalities' that formed the proper objects of God's saving work in Christ. Such institutions imbedded systemic selfishness that left societies broken. Taking the Kingdom of Evil seriously as a human phenomenon placed struggle against the hells of our own making as central to Christian faith. Hell was a condition of alienation and hurt in the here-and-now for which we were all culpable. It was all that opposed the coming of God's kingdom into which we were invited to be part. It was a condition which we were all called to fight with the indestructible and indefatigable hope of the gospel.

Rauschenbusch teaches us that we are called to hope, even in crisis. The basic Christian hope, even when faced with hells of our own making, is the ideal of 'the true human society'. By this ideal human society, Rauschenbusch meant a fellowship of justice, equality and love. For Rauschenbusch, such social hope was undergirded by the promise of God to make all things new at the end. At heart, the hell that should trouble Christians was the one that humanity created, in all its manifold and insidious cultural, social, political and economic forms. Christ came to empty those hells in the saving act of his life, death and resurrection.

Populism is a crisis. It is a danger to which we must respond. A re-formed notion of hell can give us the language and tools to do so. We can combine the perspective of the merciful hearted, the modern imagining of this-worldly calamities as hell, and the social theology of people like Walter Rauschenbusch. This synthesis can shape a retrieved apocalyptic imagination. In this apocalyptic imagination, hell describes alienation from God and from one another. This alienation is catastrophic and the harbinger of terror in the here-and-now. It is a condition rather than a place. Conditions can change; they are not everlasting. We can work with the grain of God's grace to unveil what and where hell is. By joining in with the unfolding of the kingdom of heaven, we can empty hell of any substantial reality. We can have hope.

Our hope must, however, also have a degree of self-aware caution.

Emptying hell does not start or end with our own unaided action. It is Christ's 'descent into hell' that inaugurates the end of 'hell on earth'. In his descent into hell, Jesus bore its fullness and overcame it. It will be Christ's return at the end of the ages that consummates what God has begun in history. We are called to share in Christ's 'harrowing of hell' as part of the 'now but not yet' quality of the kingdom of heaven that has broken into our world. Rauschenbusch's vision of hope was idealistic but also realistic. 'We shall demand perfection', he wrote, 'but we shall never get it.'[22] Nevertheless, as Christians anticipate the fullness of new life in the kingdom of heaven, the imperative to work with God in the imperfections of the here-and-now remained. This was a vision of hope conditioned by humility. This is the hope to which we are still called and through which we can endure. 'By demanding [perfection]', Rauschenbusch averred, 'we shall get more than we have now' through the gracious activity of God.

Neither does emptying hell exclude God's disrupting us. We must be wary of recapitulating any 'us' versus 'them' way of thinking. An apocalyptic imagination equally unveils the ways in which we and our communities may well be part of the creation of hell for others. Populism is but one form of self-induced alienation that comes from the humiliation of others. Religious communities are another form. Humility requires reflexive self-awareness of the ways in which we are simultaneously saints and sinners. Christian communities have done terrible things across history and continue to do so. They have humiliated and degraded others based upon their religion, ethnicity, gender or sexuality. They have been complicit with systematic forms of abuse, violence, exclusion and oppression. Christian communities cannot be saved – or at least not without the disruptive Word of God healing them in radical ways beyond our imaginings.

God disrupts us with the unveiling of hell and our complicity as its architects. The hope we have must remain indexed against humility, repentance and openness. Hell arrests us with the terrible sight unveiled to us that we are dual citizens. Hell demands that we search out how we are citizens of the Kingdom of Evil as much as we are citizens of heaven.

If Sartre is right and 'hell is other people', then we must patiently, humbly and urgently let Christ unveil, descend into and dismantle the self-induced hells built upon humiliation. We must surrender ourselves to the wild currents of God's grace through an apocalyptic imagination about hell. The tides of hope will wash us on to the shores of a 'new heaven and a new earth' where 'mourning and crying and pain will be no more' (Rev. 21.4). Humility rather than humiliation will mark our lives together, opened to the wonder of one another through the sacred art of contemplating the last things.

As we retrieve this sacred art, hell remains vital. If we do not believe in hell, then we should. Only then can we join God in Christ and overcome it. Only then will the old world pass away and the new be born. Only then can we rejoice in the merciful heart of God who reconciles all things.

Notes

1 Dante Alighieri, *The Divine Comedy*, trans. Allen Mandelbaum, New York, London, Toronto: Everyman's Library, 1995, p. 68.

2 John Chrysostom, 'Discourses against Judaizing Christians', I.IV.1, in Edward Condon (ed.), *Death, Judgement, Heaven & Hell*, Washington, DC: The Catholic University of America Press, 2019, p. 76.

3 Paschasius of Dumium, *Questions and Answers of the Greek Fathers*, 12, in Condon (ed.), *Death, Judgement, Heaven & Hell*, p. 81.

4 Jonathan Edwards, 'The Eternity of Hell Torments' in *The Wrath of Almighty God*, Morgan, PA: Soli Deo Gratia, 1996, pp. 356–7.

5 John Furniss, *The Sight of Hell*, Dublin: James Duffy & Co., 1874, pp. 3–10, 12–21, 23–5, in Scott G. Bruce (ed.), *The Penguin Book of Hell*, New York, NY: Penguin Books, 2018, pp. 201–21.

6 W. E. Gladstone, *Studies Subsidiary to the Works of Bishop Butler*, New York, NY: Macmillan, 1896, p. 206.

7 Scott G. Bruce (ed.), *The Penguin Book of Hell*, New York, NY: Penguin Books, 2018, p. 200.

8 David Bentley Hart, *That All Shall Be Saved: Heaven, Hell & Universal Salvation*, New Haven, CT: Yale University Press, 2019, p. x.

9 Hart, *That All Shall Be Saved*, p. 1.

10 Quoted in J. W. Hanson, *Universalism: The Prevailing Doctrine Of The Christian Church During Its First Five Hundred Years*, Boston and Chicago Universalist Publishing House, 1899, p. 324.

11 Isaac the Syrian, *Isaac of Nineveh (Isaac the Syrian) The Second Part, Chapters IV–XLIII*, trans. Sebastian Brock, In aedibus Peeters, 1995, II/39, p. 13.

12 Augustine of Hippo, *Against Julian*, 12.24, in Condon (ed.), *Death, Judgement, Heaven & Hell*, p. 77.

13 Augustine of Hippo, *Continence*, 6.15, in Condon (ed.), *Death, Judgement, Heaven & Hell*, p. 76.

14 John Robinson, 'Universalism – Is it Heretical?', *Scottish Journal of Theology*, 2 2 (1949), p. 155.

15 Peter Berger, *A Rumour of Angels*, Harmondsworth: Penguin, 1971, p. 70.

16 Daniel Nilsson DeHanas, 'Sacred, Supernatural, and Apocalyptic Populism', *London School of Economics and Political Science*, 17 December 2018, https://blogs.lse.ac.uk/religionglobalsociety/2018/12/sacred-supernatural-and-apocalyptic-populism/, accessed 09.05.2024. See also Daniel Nilsson DeHanas and Marat Shterin (eds), *Religion and the Rise of Populism*, London: Routledge, 2020.

17 Jean-Paul Sartre, *Sartre on Theatre*, trans. Frank Jellinek, New York: Pantheon, 1976, p. 199.

18 Walter Rauschenbusch, *A Theology for the Social Gospel and Other Writings*, Macon, GA: Mercer University Press, 2018, p. 93.

19 Rauschenbusch, *A Theology for the Social Gospel*, p. 34.

20 Rauschenbusch, *A Theology for the Social Gospel*, p. 42.

21 Rauschenbusch, *A Theology for the Social Gospel*, pp. 48–63.

22 Walter Rauschenbusch, *Christianizing the Social Order*, New York, NY: MacMillan, 1914, pp. 29, 126.

3

Judgement

This is my fear, and I live with it day and night. The thought of glory on the one side and of punishment on the other does not let me breathe.
(Gregory of Nazianzus, c. 329–390)

Love has been perfected among us in this: that we may have boldness on the day of judgement, because as he is, so are we in this world. There is no fear in love, but perfect love casts out fear; for fear has to do with punishment, and whoever fears has not reached perfection in love.
(1 John 4.17–18)

It is now an open secret
Black people do not have
Chips on their shoulders,
They just have injustice on their backs
And justice on their minds,
And now we know that the road to liberty
Is as long as the road from slavery.
(Benjamin Zephaniah, 1958–2023)[1]

'Judgement' is the sinew that connects 'heaven' and 'hell'. Like heaven and hell, however, judgement often sits uneasily with our modern sensibilities. It seems another inauspicious tradition to recover. Once again, the prospects seem bleak for judgement as part of retrieving the sacred art of contemplating the four last things.

When we talk about judgement in theological terms, we most typically mean the 'last judgement'. The last judgement describes the final judgement God metes out at the end of the ages. It is a basic article of Christian faith: the Nicene Creed proclaims that Christ 'will come again in glory to judge the living and the dead, and his kingdom will have no end.'

The most common interpretation of the last judgement in the Christian tradition has been that it involves a dual outcome. Some will receive eternal life. Others will receive eternal damnation. God will weigh the outcome for each person according to the nature of the lives they have lived or the faith they have. The last judgement hangs over all of us. As St Ambrose in the fourth century summarized, 'in the day of judgement, our works will either succour us or plunge us into the depths, like men weighted with millstone'.[2]

The basic scriptural text behind the notion of a dual outcome was the parable of the judgement of the nations in Matthew 25.31–46. There, 'when the Son of Man comes in his glory … he will separate people one from another as a shepherd separates the sheep from the goats'. Christ will declare some 'blessed by my Father' and reward them with the 'kingdom prepared for you from the foundation of the world'. Others will be declared 'accursed' and sent 'into the eternal fire prepared for the devil and his angels'.

In this passage, the Gospel of Matthew likely had in mind the judgement of the nations based upon how they treat Christians. It did not take much imagination, however, to stretch it into a vision of a universal judgement to come upon the morality of human acts wholesale. Such a universal judgement certainly appeared to be implied in the vision of the last judgement in Revelation 21. There, a triumphant Christ would reward the good with the 'water of life' but cast the unrighteous into 'the lake that burns with fire and sulphur, which is the second death' (Rev. 21.8).

The dual outcome of the last judgement was sometimes thought of in different terms. Some have pictured the negative outcome of the last judgement as involving annihilation rather than punishment. The few who have advocated this have looked to scriptural texts to justify it. For example, 2 Maccabees

7.14 speaks of only the righteous rising from the grave. Others remain in the non-existence of death. Likewise, 1 Corinthians 3.11–15 talks about a purifying fire that destroys only that which is worthless rather than the whole person. This view has always proved a minority report, however, and was often dismissed as heretical.

The same was true for those who have pictured the last judgement as involving the universal salvation of all creation. As we saw in the last chapter, for the universalists, there was only one outcome of the last judgement: the restoration of all things at the end of the ages. Such universalism did not win the day in terms of how the Christian tradition understood the last judgement. As we have seen, St Augustine of Hippo developed the idea of the fittingness of the last judgement since it expressed the divine quality of justice. Divine justice demanded that God punishes sins and rewards virtues. 'The good will be separated from the wicked', Augustine wrote, by God who is a 'just Judge'.[3] Augustine's thought soon became the majority view. Any ideas of universal salvation became relegated to a marginal view of suspect orthodoxy.

The firm and unwavering commitment that emerged to a dual outcome of heaven and hell gave a sharp and cutting edge to the last judgement in the minds of believers. 'When I hear the dread sentence of God', wrote St Basil, 'I know not how to fear sufficiently the greatness of His wrath.'[4] The fate of the soul was precarious. St Ambrose warned that 'for a few moments of a good work or a degenerate deed the scale [of divine judgement] often inclines to this side or that'.[5] 'In God's judgement,' warned Tertullian, 'even secret thoughts and unfulfilled violations can be accounted sinful.'[6] 'The judgement will be awesome,' declared St Cyril of Jerusalem, 'the sentence an occasion to dread.'[7]

The last judgement became an occasion for terror. Western images typically depicted its dual outcome in bleak terms that trouble the modern viewer. Michelangelo in the Sistine Chapel, for example, showed Christ stretching out his hand, ready to execute justice. On one side, devils drag dolorous sinners down to hell. On the other side, angels lift the virtuous up to heaven. Hieronymus Bosch painted a triptych of the last judgement even more sombre in its tone. The left panel showed the fall of the parents of humankind and their expulsion from the Garden of Eden. The central panel showed Christ at the top surrounded by the saints, delivering judgement from heaven. Far greater in number are people below on the earth. Demons exact cruel punishments on them. The damned are burned, impaled, force fed and tortured. They spill out into the right panel, where the devil sits enthroned, and the punishments of the souls in perdition continue. Hell is well populated, whereas heaven is sparse. These images reflected a commonly held sense that 'the gate is narrow and the road is hard that leads to life, and there are few who find it' (Matt. 7.14).

As such, the last judgement became a source of fear rather than hope. It would bring reward only for a few; the many would be condemned for ever. People should tremble in the fear of God.

As traditional Christian belief has waned in the western world, far fewer people than before are concerned with the last judgement. 'Judgement' evokes a sense of being 'judgemental'. That is now seen as a negative quality of overweening self-righteousness that damns those seen as 'impure'. For everyone else, those who are judgemental are people to avoid.

Even if we think about the last judgement at all, the fear it might create remains shadowy and distant. After all, the last judgement refers to an indefinite future state. Even for those who believe in it, it might feel abstracted from everyday life. It simply serves as a reminder that actions have consequences in this life or the next. The root of this abstraction comes from the scepticism about the last things in the Enlightenment, the intellectual movement of the seventeenth and eighteenth centuries that emphasized reason over tradition. Among those who retained the idea, thinkers such as John Locke and Immanuel Kant rendered the last judgement solely in abstract terms of underpinning moral responsibility. Others now go even further. Many might dismiss the last judgement as an illusion and mere psychological tool to produce moral behaviours obedient to the teaching of the Church. Like the heaven and hell it connects, the last judgement is suspicious and morally problematic.

It is impossible to deny that the Christian tradition has involved a regrettable and suspicious turn to terror in relation to the last judgement. The idea is wheeled out by those who perceive themselves as pious to condemn those they consider wicked. Such talk seems to belong to religious cranks and fanatics. Both aspects render the last judgement as unattractive and outmoded to most people.

Traditions can be ended, however. Alternative traditions can be unveiled. If we are to restore the credibility of the last judgement as part of retrieving a sacred art of contemplating the last things, we must begin by exploring these alternatives. What we will discover is an alternative vision of hope. This vision bears upon the present world as an urgent concern. It can shape the here-and-now in the light of a better future. As we will see, it can shape an apocalyptic imagination about judgement that informs among other things critical calls for racial justice.

To unveil an alternative understanding of the last judgement we do well to begin with the Scriptures.

In the Scriptures, the last judgement was broadly something to be anticipated with eagerness, hope and joy. It was not to be feared. Amid the crises and tumults of the world, Christ declared, 'Surely I am coming soon!' (Rev. 22.20). His return would destroy the devil, death and hell or *Hades* (Rev. 20.7–10). Christ would restore the heavens and the earth as a new creation (Rev. 21.1–4). The second coming of Christ at the end of the ages was to be prayed for earnestly as a result. 'Our Lord, come!' was one of the earliest of Christian prayers (1 Cor. 16.22). It was a cry leaning into the promise that God would come with mercy to save, heal and restore a broken world.

Any reference to judgement seen in the Scriptures must be parsed through this major note of hope. That does not mean that justice must not be served. Rather, it means that the hope of mercy must condition what we think constitutes the justice of divine judgement. 'Neither is mercy without judgement, nor judgement without mercy,' wrote St Basil in the fourth century.[8] Above all, 'mercy triumphs over judgement', the Scriptures declared (James 2.13).

As we will see, the substance of judgement in the Scriptures was salvation, not condemnation. Judgement aimed at healing and restoration under God. It formed an apocalyptic imagination that unveiled injustice and gave a clarion call to join in with God's work of restoring right relations. That restoration would be completed by God's justice at the end of the ages for the good of all (Acts 3.21; Col. 1.20; 1 Cor. 15.24–28). Only those dispositions and conditions that were evil would be annihilated, leaving behind restored right relationships.

In the Hebrew Scriptures, while human beings could be appointed as 'judges', the primary reference for judgement was God. God was 'a God of judgement' (Isa. 30.18), or even 'the God of judgement' (Mal. 2.17). Abraham called God 'the judge of all the earth' (Gen. 28.25). Judgement described the natural identity and activity of God (Deut. 32.4; Isa. 40.14; Jer. 8.7). Judgement formed 'the foundation of his throne' (Ps. 97.2). God was seen as loving judgement (Isa. 61.8).

The character of God as Judge was one shaped by hope, mercy and repair. In biblical Hebrew, the word for 'judge' (*shaphat*) could also mean 'save'. Across the Hebrew Scriptures, God was variously cast as the One who saves after judging, saves instead of judging, or saves in judging. Following an invasion, for example, Jehoshaphat prayed that 'if disaster comes upon us, the sword, judgement, or pestilence, or famine, we will ... cry to you in our distress, and you will hear and save' (2 Chron. 20.9). 'The Lord is our judge', proclaimed the prophet Isaiah, '... he will save us' (Isa. 33.22). While often God's saving acts were focused on Israel as God's chosen people, they were also expanded to include all of creation. 'Your righteousness is like the mighty mountains,' the psalmist declared, 'your judgements are like the great deep; you save humans and animals alike, O Lord' (Ps. 36.6). Judgement was God's work of social and personal restoration in the messy and broken realities of flesh and blood communities.

Within this context, the God who was Judge was also just, loved justice, and enjoined human beings to imitate God's mercy in doing justice (Micah 6.8). As the modern theologian Isabelle Hamley writes, 'the Bible is steeped in the language of justice, and the people of God, throughout the Old and New Testaments, are called to do justice as a central aspect of their vocation'.[9] Judgement, then, was an action rather than a punitive sentence. It entailed what the medieval theologian Thomas Aquinas called the 'act of justice'.[10] The link between judgement and justice was absolute. 'Follow justice and justice alone', God told his chosen people (Deut. 16.20).

The Hebrew word for justice was *mishpat*. *Mishpat* was either a judgement rendered, or the situation effected by a judgement. The word had legal roots. In theological terms, however, it was associated with soft qualities like love, faith, mercy and truth (e.g. Ps. 36.5; 89.14; Ez. 29.21; Hos. 22.19). As such, *mishpat* joined a sense of the rule of law with clemency and interpersonal healing. Judgement and justice were one breath. Judgement-as-justice sought reconciliation and restoration rather than mere retribution.

Mishpat or justice aimed at *tsedeqa*, which is commonly translated as 'righteousness'. *Tsedeqa* was not, however, a personal quality, such as the English word 'righteous' implies. It did not describe the piety or virtue of an individual. *Tsedeqa* meant doing the right thing. 'Righteousness' described right actions, rather than the moral character of a person. 'Happy are those who observe justice', the psalmist wrote, and 'who *do* righteousness at all times' (Ps. 106.3; my italics). To know God is to 'do justice' (Jer. 7.8–10) and God accordingly loved 'the person of justice and righteousness' (Ps. 11.7; 37.38; 45.8).

The righteousness that God's judgement enjoined had a social character. Righteousness described right relations between people and God. Justice was concerned with righteousness insofar as it aimed at systemic fairness. This matrix explains why the Hebrew scriptural notions of justice so often emphasized the condition of widows, orphans, strangers and the poor (e.g. Deut. 15.7, 11; cf. James 1.27). God as Judge had what modern liberation theologians call a 'preferential option for the poor' or the vulnerable. God called the people of God to model their society on this preferential option.

Justice was based upon the inherent dignity of human beings as made in God's image and likeness (Gen. 1.26). Actions that eroded or denied that image evoked the need for judgement to restore right relations or righteousness. Justice was not abstract, then, but expressed itself in concrete acts of deliverance for those who were in some way marginalized or oppressed (Ex. 3.7–8). Justice was interpersonal and rooted in the messy realities of human societies. Justice within the community was a marker of holiness, which was sharing in the character and life of God. 'Be holy because I am holy,' God declared (Lev. 19.2). The examples of what sharing in holiness looked like were summarized as 'love your neighbour' and 'love the stranger' as yourself (Lev. 19.18, 24). A caring and inclusive community of right, fair and just relations was the character of being holy.

The goal of judgement, justice and righteousness was peace. The English word 'peace' translates the Hebrew *shalom*. Such peace was not the mere absence of conflict. *Shalom* described the flourishing of human beings in all areas of life together under God (such as in Isa. 12.16–17). *Shalom* was the moral order of the universe established by divine wisdom from the beginning of time (Prov. 8.22–36). It depended upon the right ordering of relations between human beings, creation and God. In the scriptural imagination, *shalom* flowed out of divine wisdom into the busy centres of human activity, calling for justice to be done such that human flourishing under God could flower (Prov. 1.20; 3.17; 8.2–3).

In the Hebrew Scriptures, then, judgement was not the blind weighing of merits and faults outside of time. It was not concerned with eternal rewards and punishments. Rather, judgement was socially situated. It attended to the messy realities of the here-and-now. It looked for healing and hope as a present condition. It was a divine quality that God's followers were called to imitate. Judgement was a positive and dynamic way of living. Through it people lived, as it were, the life of God.

Judgement revolved around doing the right thing and protecting the vulnerable. It was the act of justice that opened the prospect of peace. It was joining in with the work of God already at play in the fabric of the cosmos and the heart of human community. The more cataclysmic visions of a 'last judgement' that began to emerge in the later writings of the Hebrew Scriptures must be seen through this lens of hope (e.g. Dan. 7.9; Isa. 24.21; Joel 3.14). God was both the origin and the end of judgement who would bring about final and complete justice for the 'healing of the nations' (Rev. 22.2; cf. Isa. 41.1).

As we turn to the New Testament, Jesus embodied and showed God's way of doing justice. The Greek word for 'justice' was *krisis*, from which we get the English word 'crisis'. *Krisis* also meant 'judgement'. It had the sense of separating the morally praiseworthy act from that which deserved condemnation. *Krisis* was a decisive moment of reckoning that sought restoration of right or just relations. In the Gospels, Jesus taught and healed as part of rendering *krisis* or justice/judgement. This was the good news of Christ.

Matthew's Gospel makes clear the restorative quality of Christ's whole life as the coming of God's justice in flesh and blood. Matthew quotes from Isaiah to describe Jesus as God's 'beloved' who would 'proclaim justice [*krisis*] to the Gentiles', 'bring justice [*krisis*] to victory', and in whose 'name the Gentiles will hope' (Matt. 12.17–20). Jesus represented the *krisis* that disturbed injustice and opened a new, divine way of life based upon the righting of relationships.

The first coming of Jesus brought hope, then, rather than fear. The justice or judgement that he heralded was conditioned by mercy and the prospect of salvation, a word that itself means 'deliverance' or even 'healing'. 'God did not send the Son into the world to condemn the world,' as John's Gospel put it, 'but in order that the world might be saved through him' (John 3.17). Jesus proclaimed, 'I came not to judge the world, but to save the world' (John 12.47). For those who had faith in Jesus through the Holy Spirit, redemption rather than retribution was possible (1 Cor. 3.11–15). While people were worthy of condemnation, sharing in the life, death and resurrection of Christ gave forgiveness and a new way of life as a gift (1 Thess. 5.9–10; Rom. 3.24–25).

The 'kingdom of God' – rather than 'judgement' in a negative sense – was the keynote of what Jesus taught. In the Gospel of Luke, Jesus proclaimed that he inaugurated God's reign of justice (Luke 4.18–19). Adapting the opening verses of Isaiah 61, Jesus identified himself as the Chosen One anointed by the Holy Spirit to proclaim the coming of God's justice or 'the year of the Lord's favour'. Talk of bringing 'good news to the poor', releasing 'the captives' and letting 'the oppressed go free' made it clear that Jesus brought liberation. The way Jesus used Isaiah 61 also evoked an earlier passage from Isaiah 58.6–7 where the prophet spoke of God's call for justice:

> Is not this the fast that I choose:
>> to loose the bonds of injustice,
>> to undo the thongs of the yoke,
> to let the oppressed go free,
>> and to break every yoke?

The kingdom of God and its justice was good news. As we have seen in the chapter on 'heaven', the kingdom of God was linked to dwelling in the person of Christ such that the power of God transformed human societies. This was justice in concrete action.

The kingdom of God was also bad news for that which opposed it. It rejected all that opposed the coming of that reign of justice. It involved judgement insofar as it unveiled that opposition, condemned it, and sought healing from it. Another Greek biblical word linked to *krisis* was *krima*. *Krima* referred to the result of a particular judgement, such as blessing or pain. Jesus brought judgement (*krima*) on that which eroded justice. Without contradiction, then, Jesus proclaimed, 'I came into this world for judgment [*krima*] so that those who do not see may see, and those who do see may become blind' (John 9.39). 'I judge no one,' Jesus declared, but added: 'Yet even if I do judge, my judgement is valid' (John 8.15–16). Thus, for example,

Jesus condemned (*krima*) the scribes who 'have the best seats in the synagogues' but 'devour widows' houses' (Matt. 12.38–40; Matt. 23.14; Luke 20.47).

Christ was the sole criterion of judgement, the divine Judge against whom the morality of actions could be judged (Matt. 25.31–46). In his role as Judge, however, Christ was also the criterion of mercy through whom the whole of creation without exception would be reconciled through purifying judgement (Col. 1.20). He warned people 'do not judge [*krima*], so that you may not be judged' (Matt. 7.1–5). Judgement [*krima*] only truly originates in the righteousness of God.

Christ's concern, then, was not with condemnation as such but with righteousness. The Greek word for 'righteousness' was *dikaiosuné*. That word and its cognates occur over 300 times in the New Testament. Like its Hebrew equivalent *tsedeqa*, the word does not refer to some special personal piety or virtue, but means doing the right thing. It is the practical expression of justice. It focuses on right action in the communal sphere. It describes the 'making right' of relationships with people, creation and God. To be 'righteous' is to 'act rightly'. To be 'righteous' is to 'act justly'. Such just action shares in God's character as 'righteous' or 'just' (Rom. 1.17). The 'kingdom of God' established 'right relations' or 'righteousness' between people. That included the unrighteous, the 'lost sheep' whom Jesus came to save.

To act justly was costly, but it was also hopeful.

In the Beatitudes, Jesus warned that the 'righteous' would be 'persecuted' (Matt. 5.10). If such righteousness (*dikaiosuné*) referred to personal virtue, that would be difficult to understand. After all, virtuous people typically receive praise, not persecution. If we translate the passage more properly as 'happy are those who are persecuted in the cause of right' (as does the *Jerusalem Bible*), it makes more sense. Those who challenge oppressive forces undoubtedly turn that force upon themselves. This indeed led to Jesus' own death.

Likewise, in the Beatitudes Christ promised that those who 'hunger and thirst for righteousness' would have their desire 'filled' (Matt. 5.6). Again, such 'righteousness' (*dikaiosuné*) was not a character trait. What Jesus meant is that people will be 'happy' insofar as they strive for 'what is right'. Their happiness would be in God as the guarantor of ultimate justice. They would 'inherit the kingdom of God' as a gift which unfolds in their communities. 'Doing right' meant acting like Christ as the embodiment of divine justice. 'Let the same mind be in you that was in Christ Jesus,' wrote St Paul, the Christ who 'emptied himself, taking the form of a servant' (Phil. 2.4–7).

'Judgement' formed another word for 'hope', then, in the New Testament. It was a hard-won, realistic and defiant hope. As such, the last judgement envisaged in the New Testament was seen in relation to the cross and resurrection. It was an Easter phenomenon that showed that God's justice was on the side of the victim and promised restitution. The 'mind of Christ' that St Paul admonished believers to imitate involved sharing in how Christ 'became obedient to the point of death – even death on a cross' (Phil. 2.8). If Jesus inaugurated a divine reign of justice, he was also the victim of a gross injustice in the crucifixion. 'He the Judge was judged,' exclaimed the *Apostolic Constitutions* written in the late fourth century. The judgement rendered upon the innocent Christ was a mockery of human justice. On the cross, 'all the evil impulses of the human race came to focus in [Jesus]', as Fleming Rutledge puts it.[11] God stood in solidarity with human brokenness on the cross. He judged deadly injustice. From the cross Christ then 'descended' into the 'hells' of our own making. Christ lifted us up from the inferno of human injustices. In the resurrection, God's love, mercy and justice began to make all things new. God's love was stronger than injustice. The resurrected Christ bore a new and imperishable body through whom all creation would be reconciled for all time.

The New Testament witnessed to the hope of such a last judgement, testifying that insofar as we are incorporated into Christ's body through the Holy Spirit, Christ has done away with condemnation and death. Instead, Christ's judgement would lead people towards peace and wholeness (Rom. 8.2, 6,

15). That was the end of justice. Christ alone was the decisive 'first and the last, and the living one', the beginning and end of justice (Rev. 1.17–18). To borrow a phrase from Martin Luther King Jr, in Christ we can see that the 'arc of the moral universe is long, but it bends toward justice'.[12]

Overall, the New Testament pointed people to share in what the womanist theologian Delores Williams called Christ's 'ministerial vision',[13] which gives a new promise of 'righteousness', understood as 'right relations'. 'Jesus came to show life', wrote Williams, '– to show redemption through a perfect ministerial vision of righting relations.'[14] For Williams, redemption calls us 'to participate in this ministerial vision of righting relations'.[15] The cross represented 'the evil of humankind trying to kill the ministerial vision of life in relation that Jesus brought humanity'.[16] The resurrection shows God's justice is stronger than any human injustice.

The New Testament 'ministerial vision of righting relations' opens a new vista of possibility and challenge. We are remade by the life, death and resurrection of Jesus. The last judgement is a refining (even a painful and scarring) process of becoming who God calls us to be in Christ as the Judge who saves. We are to reject fear and embrace hope in the biblical vision of judgement-as-justice. 'For through the Spirit, by faith,' as St Paul wrote, 'we eagerly wait for the hope of righteousness' (Gal. 5.5). We are also to be 'accountable to everyone who raises questions about the hope that is in you' (1 Peter 3.15).

If 'righteousness' or 'justice' is our hope, then we must be ready to account for how we work with the grain of God's love. We must develop an apocalyptic imagination around judgement so that injustice is unveiled, even in our own communities. We must work with God to curate justice in the flesh and blood of our communities. As St Paul commended, 'just as you have always obeyed me, not only in my presence but much more now in my absence, work on your own salvation with fear and trembling, for it is God who is at work in you, enabling you both to will and to work for his good pleasure' (Phil. 2.12–13). This will make the difference between heaven and hell for us. It will give us 'boldness on the day of judgment, because as [God] is, so are we in this world' (1 John 4.17–18). The justice of judgement gives hope that, in the end, divine love wins. Such love restores right relationships.

When it comes to justice, however, hope seems in short supply in our modern world. The past few decades have seen a resurgence of protest movements against human injustice. These movements have variously had in their sights globalization, austerity measures, political oppression, climate change, or gender and racial violence and inequality. The aim of all such movements is justice. They call for the changes needed to secure it. Whatever the popularity of these protest movements, however, change feels elusive. Hope fades. Anger simmers. Divisions widen. Injustice reigns.

We desperately need to recover hope.

Retrieving the sacred art of contemplating the last things can be one resource to inspire hope and drive change. If we develop an apocalyptic imagination about judgement as the joining in with the arc of divine justice, it can feed realistic optimism. This optimism will remain realistic insofar as it acknowledges the risk and cost of justice. It will remain focused on the priority of Christ as the criterion and ultimate guarantor of justice. Christ as Judge unveils where injustice exists. He reveals the ways in which we may be complicit in it. He uncovers a more divine way of healing, restoration and new creation, should we but lean into God's grace. He discloses the hope that, in the end, God's reign of justice will prevail.

We can see what this hope may look like by focusing on racial justice as one example.

'Racial justice' refers to the systematic fair treatment of people of all races, resulting in equitable opportunities and outcomes for all. Racial justice is not about changing the minds of all racists, changing racist laws, or preventing racist acts. It looks to uproot the racist cultures and systems that give rise to racism and racist expression. Racial justice is a corporate endeavour. It names and shames racism. It also seeks the justice of a new way of life together for everyone.

Racial justice has gained popular currency through the Black Lives Matter movement of the past decade. The Black Lives Matter movement was born out of incidents of police brutality and violence against African Americans. It quickly spread, highlighting systemic racism and racial inequality across the western world, while promoting social change and anti-racism.

While the Black Lives Matter movement is new, racist violence and racial inequality are not. The modern realities of black suffering are born out of the cruel legacy of enslavement and segregation. While these have long ended, the racism and forms of racial violence that underpinned them continue as insidious forces. They continue to create systems of injustice for African Americans and other global majority heritage ethnic groups that deny equal access to positive opportunities and outcomes in life.

Racism is not exclusive, of course, to the United States of America.

One of my earliest memories in the United Kingdom was the murder of Stephen Lawrence. Stephen was a black British teenager from London. In 1993 he was murdered in a racially motivated attack while waiting for a bus. While witnesses saw five white youths attack and murder Stephen, only two were eventually prosecuted years later. Reviews of the subsequent police investigations unveiled how racism shaped the mishandling of the murder case. One report in 1998 labelled the police as institutionally racist as a result. That report led to profound cultural changes in attitudes to racism, to the law, and to police practice. Out of such terrible injustice, Stephen's mother also founded the 'Stephen Lawrence Charitable Trust' committed to the advancement of racial and social justice.

Nevertheless, recent studies have shown that 30 years later Britain is still not close to being a racially just society. Nearly a third of people from ethnic and religious minority groups reported racial discrimination in education and employment. More than a fifth of all minorities reported experience of discrimination from the police. This figure rose to 43 per cent when it came to Black Caribbean groups. More than a third of people from ethnic and religious minorities have experienced racially motivated assault. Racial injustice remains endemic.

All these examples are the visible edge of a vast subterranean experience of deeply engrained racism in the western world. The British dub poet Benjamin Zephaniah wrote a poem in 1999 entitled 'What Stephen Lawrence has taught us'. For Zephaniah, Stephen's murder unveiled a terrible racist reality in the United Kingdom. While Stephen's killers seemed to be protected by the law, black people 'have injustice on their backs/And justice on their minds.' This racist reality was sobering. 'And now we know that the road to liberty', continued Zephaniah, 'is as long as the road from slavery.'

Zephaniah rightly traced the origins of racism to slavery. Racism was at the heart of the transatlantic slave trade from the sixteenth to the nineteenth century, bound up with western colonial expansion and the emergence of capitalism.

'Race was invented', writes the Nigerian Irish academic Emma Dabiri, 'to create racist beliefs.'[17] In the early modern period, white westerners invented a supposed racial difference between 'cultured' and 'enlightened' people of European origin and those of African descent. 'White' people became seen as the epitome of culture, reason and human development, while 'non-white' people were the contrary of these things and incapable of self-government.

The invention of race gave birth to 'white supremacy' and 'white privilege'. White supremacy is the spurious idea that white people have a natural superiority to other groups. White privilege describes the disproportionate social advantage white people have in terms of access to wealth, health and opportunity because of white supremacy. As the Black theologian Willie Jennings puts it, 'the white self-sufficient man' was defined by 'possession, mastery, and control'.[18] The Black theologian James Cone wrote that 'whiteness' became a symbol of 'madmen' who were 'sick' with deluded notions of their own superiority.[19] Whiteness blinded white people, trapping them in delusions that oppressed others. 'Oppressors', observed Cone, 'are not only rendered incapable of knowing their own condition, they cannot speak about or for the oppressed.'[20]

White supremacy legitimated the economic exploitation and domination of other ethnic groups. It was the destiny of white people to subdue and control the earth and its peoples. White privilege was the natural inheritance of a superior white race. White supremacy led to crusade, conquest and colonization. It gave permission to subdue, enslave and sell other human beings as capital assets.

While explicit racism is now largely the preserve of white extremists, racism has shaped entire subterranean ways of being in the western world. The embedded habits of racism are the afterlives of slavery. We often cannot see the racist waters in which we swim and live. Even after colonialism, the racist legacy of empire casts troubling shadows over the world for people of colour to this day. Institutional and cultural racism leads to inequality of access to education, employment, justice and health. White supremacy created entire systems of oppression that destroy lives and maintain racial subordination and marginalization. The white perception of people of colour often shows both suspicion and fragility, even as white people protest they are not 'racist'. 'Whiteness looks at people of colour', writes the Korean American theologian Grace Ji-Sun Kim, 'and accuses them of cutting in line to receive unearned entitlements which white people receive without question.'[21] 'White people', Kim continues, 'believe that people of colour are lazy and want hand-outs from the government.'[22]

Alongside the material impact of racial injustice, then, the racist legacy of colonialism also has an ongoing and devastating psychological impact. The Kenyan writer Ngũgĩ wa Thiong'o writes that colonialism's 'most important area of domination was the mental universe of the colonized, the control, through culture, of how people perceived themselves and their relationship to the world'.[23] Colonialism forced assimilation into 'white' modes of being, thinking and doing. The sociologist Boaventura de Sousa Santos labels this as 'epistemicide',[24] meaning the colonial murdering of non-white and indigenous forms of knowing. White supremacy marginalizes other ethnic expressions as inferior and illegitimate. Only 'whiteness' counts. Anything else is failure.

The terrible invention of race found resources in the religious traditions of the west. Racism did not emerge in a vacuum, but has a religious character that may surprise people. We are more attuned to the way that some Christians took a lead in challenging slavery, segregation and racial injustice. We must reckon, however, with the complicity of Christianity and Christian communities in creating and sustaining racial injustice, both historically and still now. We must unveil, judge and reckon with the racist legacy of Christianity as part of working for racial justice. When allied with white power and the 'iron cage' of capitalism, Christianity became deadly.

It was not always so. In the beginning, Christian communities contained a variety of religious identities from Jewish and Gentile worlds. While there were theological and social tensions, what really mattered was the new identity created by becoming a follower of Christ. 'There is neither Jew nor Gentile,' wrote St Paul, 'neither slave nor free, nor is there male and female, for you are all one in Christ Jesus' (Gal. 3.28). The binary was between those who were 'in Christ' and those who were 'outside' the Christian faith.

This binary grew, however, into a racialized problem in the early centuries of the Church.

Even though Jesus was a Jew, Christian theology slowly but surely embraced a virulent anti-Judaism. Christianity firmly became a supersessionist religion. 'Supersessionism' comes from a verb meaning 'to set aside in favour of another'. Christianity saw itself as replacing Jews as God's Chosen People. Jews as a people were associated with legalism, whereas Christians were concerned with grace. Gentile Christians began to claim that their communities were the true Israel. Anti-Judaism led to anti-Semitism. Christians cast Jews as responsible for the death of Jesus, as subhuman, and as enemies of God and humankind. John Chrysostom for example, delivered anti-Semitic sermons in the fourth century. In eight *Homilies Against the Jews*, he labelled Jews as being Christ-killers, bestial, demonic, immoral, idolaters, cannibals, cursed and worthy of being killed. The seeds were sown for violent anti-Semitism that took hold of the European imagination in the subsequent centuries. Jews were forced to convert to Christianity, persecuted, marginalized and killed.

The racialized problem around Judaism that emerged from the early Church laid the ground for later forms of white supremacist racism. The Black theologian Willie Jennings argues that Christian anti-Judaism and anti-Semitism shaped Europe's encounter with the Americas in the early modern world. Indigenous peoples were seen in similar ways to Jews,[25] namely that they needed conversion or deserved elimination. The African American theologian J. Kameron Carter likewise links Christian supersessionism with the later colonial conquest of Africa.[26] Like the Jews, African people were seen by western white colonialists as less than human and by missionaries as in need of conversion. Racist violence underpinned both perspectives. 'White Christianity', explains Grace Ji-Sun Kim, 'told the rest of the world to admire white people, culture, history and identity', and so, 'as white Christianity spread, it created distorted identities and perceptions of people of colour around the globe'.[27] While such racism is deeply un-Christian, it was Christianity that fertilized it. Far from bringing Christ to the world, missionaries 'brought these territories under the cold, cruel, and destructive domination of the white race', as the twentieth-century French philosopher Simone Weil put it.[28]

In these contexts, sacred texts were read in a racist light and became a warrant for white supremacy and slavery. A favourite text used to justify slavery was Genesis 9.18–27. In that story, Noah passes out drunk. While his sons Shem and Japheth avert their eyes and cover their father's shame, Ham does not. When he awakes, Noah curses Ham's son Canaan and his descendants to be the 'lowest of slaves'. This story probably originated to justify the Hebrews' subjection of Canaanites as they took over the land as their own. In subsequent centuries, however, the story was overlaid with racial overtones. Folk etymology erroneously linked the name 'Ham' with 'dark' or 'brown' skin. Canaan became dropped from the story. The 'curse of Ham' was invented. Ham was made black. His descendants were made Africans. In Jewish, Christian and Islamic medieval thought, 'blackness' became a marker or even a curse of sin. The medieval explanation that black Africans, as the 'sons of Ham', were cursed and 'blackened' by their sins gave a scriptural warrant for the slave trade of the later centuries.

Anything in sacred texts that suggested racism was not a proper attitude was elided. Texts that might incite slaves to rebel were hidden. Missionaries in 1807 published, for example, *Parts of the Holy Bible, selected for the use of the Negro Slaves, in the British West-India Islands*. It was intended for use among enslaved Africans in the British West Indies. Ninety per cent of the Hebrew Scriptures and 50 per cent of the New Testament did not appear. The curated text excluded passages that spoke about equality in Christ (such as Gal. 3.28) and emphasized texts that legitimated slavery (such as Eph. 5.6).

The afterlives of slavery live on in 'white Christianity' to this day, even if we might not want to believe it. White Christianity shapes the global experience of Christians and continues to silence global majority heritage voices.

In our modern world, hope for racial justice does not begin with silence. It begins with listening to two kinds of voices.

First, hope involves listening and learning from those whose voices are taken away by white supremacy and its enduring legacy.

Second, hope also involves listening to the Holy Spirit who draws us into the righteousness of Christ (Rom. 8.9–10). The righteousness of Christ delivers a piercing but healing 'judgement'.

These human voices, woven with the voice of God, speak of what restoration and healing will look like. They speak into the racist reality in which we find ourselves. They speak of what judgement as racial justice entails. They speak of the righting of relations. These disruptive voices demand our complete conversion to the good news of Christ, who heralds divine justice breaking into the messiness of the world. Listening to these voices cultivates an apocalyptic imagination around 'judgement' that gives us hope for racial justice and leaning into a ministerial vision of righting relationships.

Let us turn to these voices now.

The kind of human voices we need to listen to can be found in what is known as 'Black theology', an American movement that began in the 1960s and which has subsequently taken on international forms.

'Black' in 'Black theology' refers to two things. First, it refers to the pigmentation of skin, the physiological trait of 'blackness' that those who produce such theology might have. Second, it also refers to what the South African theologian Nyameko Pityana calls 'one's attitude and action toward the liberation of the oppressed black people from white racism'.[29]

In turn, what the 'theology' in 'Black theology' refers to is perhaps best captured by a definition offered by the 'father' of Black theology, James Cone. For Cone, 'theology' in a Black context meant the 'rational study of the being of God in the world in light of the existential situation of an oppressed community, relating the forces of liberation to the essence of the gospel, which is Jesus Christ'.[30]

In other words, Black theology speaks from within the experience of 'blackness', speaks about the experience of racism, and speaks for an experience of healing and wholeness for all peoples. Thus, while Black theology starts from 'black' experiences, it pertains to everyone who works for racial justice. As Cone put it, 'blackness' is a 'symbol for all people who participate in the liberation of man from oppression'.[31]

Black theology offers conceptual resources from within Christianity to judge white supremacy. It also helps us understand how to develop restorative racial justice that leads to righteousness or right relations under Christ as part of an apocalyptic imagination.

The roots of Black theology were in the experiences of people from the African diaspora created by the transatlantic slave trade. Enslaved Africans in the Americas latched on to the subversive aspects of the Christianity into which they had been forcibly converted. The Bible was read from the black perspective of slavery. Biblical stories of liberation from slavery like the Exodus narrative became sources of hope. The last things such as 'heaven' offered a defiant way of speaking (or singing) hope into the present. 'Hell' and 'judgement' similarly gave a language to condemn injustices suffered and express a desire for a different future to be experienced soon.

Black theology develops this insistence of 'slave theology' on the last things. For Black theology, it is a 'white lie' that the last things are about some deferred, otherworldly reality. Black theology insists that the future can become present, forcing change in the world here-and-now with a charged vision of hope. The central feature of the last things is divine judgement on all that leads to death or life, hell or heaven, in our lives. An apocalyptic imagination leans into that divine judgement and concerns itself with racial injustice, especially as it intersects with class, gender, sexuality and age. Resistance against racism in all of its manifold forms is one way of sharing in the 'divine judgement' of evil imaged in apocalyptic texts such as Revelation.

We may struggle to know what an apocalyptic imagination about judgement might look like for us and our communities in relation to racial justice. Black theology again offers much help. Its voices call us to reflect upon, repent and repair the ravages of racism so that relationships might be renewed.

Black theology signals that the starting point is self-awareness. Communities need to critique 'whiteness'. They must become conscious of how it implicitly shapes the lives of white people in terms of white privilege. That also unveils how white privilege misshapes black lives in terms of disadvantage.

Black theology also signals that self-awareness then needs to shape the practices of the Christian faith. We need to reread the Bible to become more aware of the perspective of the oppressed. We need to hear and learn from diverse voices from within and beyond our community. We need to develop new forms of worship attentive to justice around race, class, gender, age and sexuality. Listening, learning and liturgical formation will prepare us to form coalitions for change.

Finally, Black theology reminds us that self-awareness and faithful practices must issue in the reparative actions of racial justice. From the raised consciousness shaped by reflection, prayer and worship, we can seek actions to restore right relations otherwise marred by the afterlives of slavery and racism. These actions may well be disruptive and uncomfortable. Repair begins with repentance. Repentance requires honesty, and honesty hurts. It requires humility and for people to put themselves in the vulnerable position of being judged and needing forgiveness. Forgiveness can only be asked for in good faith when we also make a pledge to take steps to repair things. That repair is the substance of justice. Reparative justice is an approach to justice that aims to repair the harm done to victims directly or vicariously through a negative legacy. The reparative work of justice is costly, both on an emotional and in a structural and financial sense. Reparations are an integral part of forgiveness insofar as they are part of healing and restoring right relations. People of faith need to wrestle with repentance as more than easy lip-service. Repentance will only result in repair and racial justice if there is redistribution of opportunities beyond white privilege. Otherwise, we remain under judgement.

Listening to these human voices about racial justice is one half of the story. We must also learn to listen together for the Holy Spirit.

The Holy Spirit was given to the Church at Pentecost (Acts 2.1–13). In the Pentecost story, the Spirit enabled the followers of Christ to speak the languages of all the 'God-fearing Jews from every nation under heaven' who were gathered in Jerusalem. This crowd included a diverse range of ethnic identities from the Middle East, Africa and Asia. As he preached on Pentecost, St Peter quoted the prophet Joel and testified to the crowd that the pouring out of the Holy Spirit 'on all flesh' signalled the 'coming of the great and glorious day of the Lord' (Acts 2.17–21).

Pentecost was the pure and liberating act of the Spirit. It revealed how the Holy Spirit draws believers into unity without enforcing uniformity (1 Cor. 12.13–14; Eph. 4.1–6). It disrupted – as it still does – the divisions we create, including that of race. It enfolds us into Christ and a new way of life together under God (Rom. 8.15; Gal. 4.5). The Holy Spirit delivers righteousness (i.e., right relations), peace, joy and hope – the new realities of justice (Rom. 8.10; 14.17; Gal. 5.5). It opens hearts to one another. It restores communication. It builds a radically new community marked by love and wrought by justice in the present. The Spirit does not erase the wounds of the present. Rather, just as the resurrected Christ bears the wounds of crucifixion, the English theologian Selina Stone reminds us that 'the Spirit calls us to see and even touch the scars' of racism.[32] Indeed, the scars, as the Spirit invites us to touch them, 'remind us of the work of God which continues to be needed in the world'.[33]

If we are to retrieve an apocalyptic imagination about the last judgement, we need to restore Pentecost as our daily reality. As a sixth-century African author preached:

> If someone should say to one of us: 'You received the Holy Spirit, why then do you not speak in all languages?', we should answer: 'I do speak in all languages, for I am a member of the body of Christ, the Church, which speaks all languages.'[34]

Letting all languages be spoken – and learning to speak racial justice – is how we share in the disruptive activity of the Holy Spirit. At the end of the ages, the fire of the Spirit will 'test what sort of work each has done' (1 Cor. 3.13). That refining fire will not be without challenge or cost, yet it will be full of hope. The fire which both burns and saves is the Spirit of Christ, Judge and Saviour. 'The builder will suffer loss', St Paul continued; but yet 'the builder will be saved, but only as through fire' (1 Cor. 3.15). The Spirit unveils justice and instils the hope we need to see it unfurl. In this Spirit, all peoples will be saved through the mercy of Christ at the last judgement.

Notes

1 Benjamin Zephaniah, 'What Stephen Lawrence has taught us', first published in *The Guardian*, 24 February 1999, https://www.theguardian.com/uk/1999/feb/24/lawrence.ukcrime3, accessed 09.05.2024; subsequently published in Benjamin Zephaniah, *Too Black, Too Strong*, Hexham: Bloodaxe Books, 2001. Used by permission.

2 St Ambrose, *Letters*, 15, in Edward Condon (ed.), *Death, Judgement, Heaven & Hell*, Washington, DC: The Catholic University of America Press, 2019, p. 40.

3 Augustine of Hippo, *City of God*, 20.30, and *Selected Sermons*, 60.10, in Condon (ed.), *Death, Judgement, Heaven & Hell*, pp. 30, 48.

4 St Basil, *On the Judgement of God (Ascetical Works)*, 45, in Condon (ed.), *Death, Judgement, Heaven & Hell*, p. 33.

5 St Ambrose, *Letters*, 15, in Condon (ed.), *Death, Judgement, Heaven & Hell*, p. 40.

6 Tertullian, *On the Soul*, 58.6, in Condon (ed.), *Death, Judgement, Heaven & Hell*, p. 41.

7 St Cyril of Jerusalem, *Catechesis*, 15.26, in Condon (ed.), *Death, Judgement, Heaven & Hell*, p. 48.

8 St Basil, *Exegetical Homilies*, 15, in Condon (ed.), *Death, Judgement, Heaven & Hell*, p. 46.

9 Isabelle Hamley, *Embracing Justice*, London: SPCK, 2021, p. 3.

10 Thomas Aquinas, *Summa Theologica*, II.II.60.1, Notre Dame, IN: Ave Maria Press, p. 1440.

11 Fleming Rutledge, *The Crucifixion: Understanding the Death of Jesus Christ*, Grand Rapids, MI: Eerdmans, 2015, p. 97.

12 Martin Luther King Jr, 'Where do we go from here?' in James M. Washington (ed.), *A Testament of Hope: The Essential Writings and Speeches of Martin Luther King Jr*, Washington, DC: HarperCollins, 1986, p. 252.

13 Delores Williams, *Sisters in the Wilderness: The Challenge of Womanist God-Talk*, Maryknoll, NY: Orbis Books, 2013.

14 Williams, *Sisters in the Wilderness*, p. 30.

15 Williams, *Sisters in the Wilderness*, p. 11.

16 Williams, *Sisters in the Wilderness*, p. 130.

17 Emma Dabiri, *What White People Can Do Next: From Allyship to Coalition*, London: Penguin, 2021, p. 31.

18 Willie Jennings, *After Whiteness: An Education in Belonging*, Grand Rapids, MI: Eerdmans, 2020, p. 29.

19 James Cone, *A Black Theology of Liberation*, Philadelphia, PA: Lippencott, 1970, p. 29.

20 Cone, *A Black Theology of Liberation*, p. 108.

21 Grace Ji-Sun Kim, *Spirit Life*, London: Darton, Longman & Todd, 2022, p. 25.

22 Kim, *Spirit Life*, p. 28.

23 Ngũgĩ wa Thiong'o, *Decolonizing the Mind: The Politics of Language in African Literature*, Oxford: James Currey/Heinemann, 1986, 2005, p. 16.

24 Boaventura de Sousa Santos, *Epistemologies of the South: Justice against Epistemicide*, New York, NY: Routledge, 2014, esp. p. 92.

25 Willie Jennings, *The Christian Imagination: Theology and the Origins of Race*, London: Yale University Press, 2010.

26 J. Kameron Carter, *Race: A Theological Account*, Oxford: Oxford University Press, 2008.

27 Kim, *Spirit Life*, pp. 26–7.

28 Simone Weil, *Letter to a Priest*, trans. A. F. Wills, London: Routledge, 2002, p. 18.

29 Nyameko Pityana, 'What Is Black Consciousness?' in Basil Moore (ed.), *Black Theology: The South African Voice*, London: C. Hurst & Co., 1973, p. 63.

30 James Cone, *Black Theology and Black Power*, New York, NY: Seabury Press, 1969, pp. 17–18.

31 Cone, *A Black Theology of Liberation*, p. 32.

32 Selina Stone, *The Spirit and the Body: Towards a womanist Pentecostal social justice ethic*, Leiden: Brill, 2023, p. 167.

33 Selina Stone, *Tarry Awhile: Wisdom from Black Spirituality for People of Faith*, London: SPCK, 2023, p. 179.

34 The reading appears in the Roman *Office of Readings* for Saturday of the 7th week of Easter, the vigil of Pentecost.

4

Death

I call heaven and earth to witness against you today that I have
set before you life and death, blessings and curses. Choose life
so that you and your descendants may live.
(Deuteronomy 30.19)

We know that we have passed from death to life because we
love one another. Whoever does not love abides in death.
(1 John 3.14)

Women of all races and black people of both genders are fast
filling up the ranks of the poor and disenfranchised. It is in our
interest to face the issue of class, to become more conscious,
to know better so that we can know how best to struggle for
economic justice.
(bell hooks, 1952–2021)[1]

Of the four last things, only 'death' is indisputable fact. After
all, death is the one certainty in life. If we are to retrieve the
sacred art of contemplating the last things, then death would
seem to be easy pickings.

Yet death is something most of us avoid thinking about. As
a society, we tiptoe around and are uneasy speaking about
our own mortality. Recent polls in the United Kingdom found
that only 21 per cent of participants had talked about their
death with someone else, while 72 per cent believed that people
are uncomfortable discussing death, dying and bereavement.
Another recent study in the United Kingdom found that nearly
90 per cent of people agreed that planning for the end of life
was essential, but only 14 per cent had formally done so. These

kinds of finding are replicated in most nations. We all know our death is inevitable. We avoid its sobering reality.

Meanwhile big business booms selling products designed to delay ageing, keep us healthy, prolong life and postpone decline and demise. Mass media and commerce encourage us to avoid contemplating our death. Even when the inevitable comes, old age, infirmity and death are all privatized and kept largely hidden from view in care homes, hospitals, hospices and undertakers. We struggle to have honest and open conversations about death, both as individuals and as a society.

In this context of denial and discomfort, communities of faith offer valuable work with people and their loved ones as they face death and bereavement. Faithful communities offer care, compassion and informal support of spiritual and practical kinds. They help people face the traumatic realities of mortality. They give ritual expressions to grief through funerals, memorial services and annual commemorations of the departed. They provide sustained pastoral care as people process loss. They offer a vision of hope that glimmers even in the dark recesses of death.

For Christians, that vision of hope is the resurrection of Jesus Christ.

From the beginning of Christianity, death was seen as fundamentally unnatural. It was part of a broken world. 'Death ... was not in nature', declared St Ambrose in the fourth century, 'but it became part of nature.'[2] The emerging Christian tradition located the entry of death in the fall of the parents of humankind. St Paul wrote that 'sin came into the world through one man [i.e., Adam], and death came through sin, and so death spread to all because all have sinned' (Rom. 5.12). Sometimes death was seen as a divine punishment for human sin. Sometimes it was seen as a divine remedy or a relief from the brokenness of the passing world prior to reunion with God.

Either way, Christ identified totally with the broken human condition when he died. He overcame death when he rose from the dead. In his life, death and resurrection, Christ became a new Adam, meaning a new parent for a renewed humankind.

St Paul wrote that 'just as one man's [i.e., Adam's] trespass led to condemnation for all, so one man's [i.e., Christ's] act of righteousness leads to justification and life for all' (Rom. 5.18). 'Death has been swallowed up in victory,' declared St Paul as he looked to the victory of Christ over death (1 Cor. 15.54). Through Christ, God vanquished death.

That victory gave Christians hope. 'As all die in Adam', proclaimed St Paul, 'so all will be made alive in Christ' (1 Cor. 15.22). At the end of time, God would cast death into the 'lake of fire' where it would be destroyed for ever (Rev. 20.14). At the end of time, 'in the twinkling of an eye ... the dead will be raised imperishable' (1 Cor. 15.52). God 'will wipe every tear' and 'death will be no more; mourning and crying and pain will be no more' (Rev. 21.4). As a result, St Augustine of Hippo encouraged believers, 'do not fear death any longer; what you fear has been conquered by the Lord'.[3]

This Christian vision of life still gives hope as we struggle with the fear, pain and grief of individual death. Yet we often miss the equally painful and destructive social nature of death in the daily fabric of living together.

When St Paul imagined the way in which humankind shares in the 'first' and 'second' Adam, he made clear that this double sharing was a corporate reality. All of humankind shares in the broken nature of the fallen Adam. All humankind dies as a result. All of humankind can share in the resurrected body of the risen Christ. All of humankind can live as a result (1 Cor. 15.22).

The social nature of death and life shapes our everyday collective realities. Death and life signal more than just our individual mortality and our post-mortem resurrection. We daily live in the social reality of death and life. We exist in the matrix of choices and ways of being that determine whether we lean into the promise of abundant life together or lean away from it through selfishness, fear, hatred, apathy and greed. We choose life or death, blessing or curse, every day.

Death does not merely describe, then, the biological fate of individuals. It also describes present human structures and powers that erode, limit and deny opportunities and outcomes in daily lives. Death describes the social brokenness that kills life in the here-and-now, in both spiritual and literal terms. As the modern theologian Marika Rose puts it, 'we create systems that are structurally violent, causing death both indirectly … and directly'. Systems kill indirectly 'by organising the world so that people cannot access the resources they need to survive'. They kill directly 'via state institutions such as the army and the police, or by … private security forces'.[4]

We are just as uneasy talking about the social reality of death as we are about our own mortality. We are disrupted and discomforted when we face up to the ways in which the world we live in is broken and kills. It requires confronting injustice – and our own complicity in it. It calls us to develop an apocalyptic imagination that might require us to see that 'the world [as we know it] doesn't need saving, but destroying', as Marika Rose provocatively suggests.[5] After all, 'our struggle', wrote St Paul, is 'against the rulers, against the authorities, against the cosmic powers of this present darkness, against the spiritual forces of evil in the heavenly places' (Eph. 6.11–13).

Not many people naturally relish such a struggle. It is far easier and more comfortable to take it for granted that the world can't be any other way than it is. The far-off promise of some otherworldly divine resolution for our social ills demands less of us than changing the world we inhabit now.

Unlike our own mortality, however, we can collectively 'choose life so that you and your descendants may live' (Deut. 30.19). Just as God set choices before the Israelites before they entered their promised land, God daily sets before us the choice between 'life and death, blessings and curses'. The choice between life and death does not simply refer to some imagined future post-mortem state for each individual. It refers just as much to the way we live life every day. We are called to oppose 'death' and 'choose life'. This involves unveiling the human structures, systems and cultures that kill, even when that involves painfully reckoning with our own complicity with them. It involves trusting in the grace of God as our security that 'life' – rather than 'death' – wins. It demands working with the grain of God's justice in the messy realities of our world.

We need to recover the choice between death and life as an urgent social imperative. If we are to retrieve the sacred art of contemplating the last things, then we must wrestle with death as part of the daily fabric of the realities we inhabit and the lives we lead. Only then might we be able to discern, choose and pursue life in abundance together through Christ (John 10.10). Only then will we live in the love of Christ. 'We know that we have passed from death to life', the Scriptures say, 'because we love one another. Whoever does not love abides in death' (1 John 3.14).

From the earliest centuries, Christianity developed a 'two ways' tradition to shape an apocalyptic imagination about choosing life every day rather than death. This tradition can form the heart of an apocalyptic imagination about death even today. It placed the choice between life and death as an ethical imperative that shaped living together in light of the righteousness or justice of God.

The 'two ways' Christian tradition grew out of Jewish roots. Following on from the divine commandment in Deuteronomy to 'choose life', Jewish teachers instilled the two ways as the heart of ethical living. The apocryphal work *Testaments of the Twelve Patriarchs*, which found its final form in the second century CE, talked about how people had to choose between 'light and darkness' or 'good and evil'. Likewise, the *Community Rule* of the Qumran community from the first century CE spoke of 'sons of light' marked by 'humility, patience, generous compassion ... and powerful wisdom which trusts entirely to the deeds of God'.[6] 'These are their ways in the world,' the *Rule* continued, namely 'to illuminate the human heart and to make straight before him all the ways of true justice.' By contrast, 'the spirit of deceit' pulled people to selfishness and atrophied just relations. The *Rule* guided its followers about how they could choose life together and reject the ways of death for the community and beyond.

This Jewish pattern of the 'two ways' informed the Christian imagination from the beginning. The first Christian example of the two ways tradition was the *Didache*, dated between the middle of the first and second centuries. The *Didache* offered a basic instruction about what it meant to live as a Christian, and the two ways were at its heart. The *Didache* began with 'there are two ways, the one of life and the one of death; the difference between them is great'.[7] The 'way of life' flowed from following the double command to love God and love neighbour. The *Didache* outlined the need to love enemies, act justly, protect the poor and cultivate lives of virtue. Life was to be chosen daily. The 'way of death' was the inversion of the 'way of life'. Death was daily to be rejected.

The two ways formed the heart of similar early Christian teaching material. By the third century, texts emerged that focused exclusively on the two ways, seeing them as integral to right living as a Christian community. From the fourth century, the two ways shaped the rise of monastic communities dedicated to forming exemplary models of service to God and neighbour. More broadly, later medieval sermons appealed to the two ways tradition to exhort listeners and their communities to make daily choices for life and reject that which led to death.

The two ways tradition saw life and death not just as biological states but also as ways of living together well under the righteousness of God. As we have seen in the last chapter, 'righteousness' (*dikaiosuné*) does not refer to some personal moral quality. Rather, it refers to acting rightly and establishing right relations. The two ways tradition formed an apocalyptic imagination which unveiled what it meant to live daily for life and against death. The apocalyptic imagination of the two ways revealed that we shape cultures and create communities which either promote life abundantly or unjustly deny life in its fullness to others.

We desperately need to retrieve the apocalyptic imagination of the two ways tradition. Death intrudes as a daily social disease in our midst in varied and insidious ways.

We can see this invidious invasion, for example, in relation to our ongoing modern economic crisis.

The international Occupy protest movement followed the financial crisis of 2008. It highlighted systemic global economic injustice and inequality. A common slogan of the Occupy protests was the phrase 'We are the 99%'. This slogan highlighted the concentration of wealth among the top 1 per cent of income earners compared to the other 99 per cent of the world's population. The Occupy protests unveiled how the gap between the haves and the have nots had become (and still remains) a chasm. The result of this injustice was more than simply economic inequality. It caused death insofar as it resulted in precarious lives for many. Such precariousness resulted in health inequities, with poorer physical and mental health for the have nots, as well as higher mortality rates.

While the Occupy protests focused on income levels, these economic disparities are ultimately the product of social class. One way, then, that we can see how systems of death intrude into our daily lives and choices is through the prism of social class, as well as the social evil of classism.

We all have a vague sense of what class means, even though sometimes people strangely deny it even exists any longer. Precisely defining, however, what class is remains more difficult.

Theorists have long debated what the concept means. What they agree on is that class is not grounded in any natural property. Class describes and explains economic, social and cultural inequality, as well as differences of power, opportunity and esteem. Class is a social, cultural and economic construct that posits a hierarchy between different classes of people. It permeates every aspect of our lives together, shaping how we view the world and one another. As the Latin American theologian Néstor Míguez writes, 'the concept of social class is the very heart of the condition of human life on the planet'.[8]

The hierarchy of class traditionally classified modern groups in broad terms of 'working', 'middle', and 'upper' classes. More recently the classifications have become ever more complex. For example, the Great British Class Survey conducted in 2011 suggested that there are now seven social classes. On the lowest end is the 'precariat class' (the poor who do not have stable income). At the top end is the 'elite class' (a small group of people who hold disproportionate wealth, privilege and power). Other social, economic and cultural gradations exist between these two poles. These include the 'traditional working class' and 'established middle class', but also 'emergent service workers', 'new affluent workers', and the 'technical middle class'.

Whatever way we stratify 'classes', what differentiates them are contrasts in economic, social and cultural capital. In other words, the financial and material assets, range of social connections, and types of education, interests and activities determine a person's social class. We could, of course, make the notion of class even more nuanced. The French sociologist Pierre Bourdieu, for example, linked class to multiple forms of 'capital': financial, technological, commercial, social, cultural and symbolic.[9] Whatever forms of capital we take into view, however, class entails differences of power, status and possibilities.

'Class' is not a neutral descriptive term. It often leads to 'classism', namely the prejudice that a person's value in society is predicated upon their social, economic or cultural standing. Class becomes value laden. These values inscribe judgements about the intellectual, social, economic and cultural worth of different classes. From ideas of class, we see various common classist depictions of 'lower' classes as dumb, rude, lewd, loungers, scroungers and scum. They are often seen as needing the paternalistic control and direction of the 'higher' classes for their own good and betterment. Their one aspiration should be to escape their lot and become like their social masters.

In short, 'class' and 'classism' describe social, economic and cultural injustices of different kinds. Fundamentally, class is not just about income levels. It is a relational term. It emerges through unfair distribution of resources and imbalances of power between classes. It produces the prejudicial stereotyping of classism to legitimate injustice. It tends towards conflict. As Karl Marx and Friedrich Engels famously declared, 'the history of all hitherto existing society is the history of class struggles'.[10]

The relational character of class reveals both its injustices and its capacity for transformative change. After all, in itself class does not inherently determine that social stratification and relationships necessarily must be imbalanced or unfair. Of course, class leads precisely to that when it produces asymmetrical relations that divide, exploit and oppress – as it typically has done. Class also, however, can be a positive source of solidarity if social relations between classes are opened to transformative symmetries of power. Oppressed classes can raise consciousness about their systemic exploitation and work for social and economic change. 'Class consciousness' can unveil injustice. It also has the potential to forge a different way of living together. Class exploitation does not need to be the way of the world.

As it exists now, however, class kills. 'A glance at the very bottom of the system', writes the contemporary theologian Joerg Rieger, 'shows how class turns into a literal struggle of life and death.'[11] Class and classism slaughters equal access to resources, opportunities, and even life itself. Increasing numbers of people face insecurity around basic access to food, housing, money, jobs and health. Recent estimates show that around 7 per cent of the British population and 10 per cent of the American population are not able to buy enough food. One in seven people in the United Kingdom, and one in 20 in America, live in inadequate housing. Seventeen per cent of the British population and 12 per cent of the American population live in absolute poverty. Meanwhile, the top 10 per cent of the British population control 43 per cent of national wealth, while the poorest 50 per cent own just 9 per cent. In America, the top 1 per cent control the same wealth as the bottom 90 per cent. For the whole world, the top 1 per cent earn around 20 per cent of the total income and own 59 per cent of all global financial assets. There are obscene levels of pay inequality across the globe. Record numbers of people face precarious employment or unemployment. Allied with decreasing levels of social mobility, people become trapped in cycles of poverty, stress and debt. It is unsurprising that the poor die much earlier on average than their rich counterparts. Recent decades show consistent widening of health inequalities and inequities in mortality rates between those at the top and those at the bottom.

The class system represents a systematic choice of systemic death rather than life in our modern societies. Its deadly consequences intersect with race and gender. Women and people of colour in the 'lower' classes face more adversity than any other group. Inequality of access to opportunities, outcomes and life trap people in systems of social, economic, cultural and literal death. Class is an urgent crisis. As the American social critic bell hooks wrote, it 'is in our interest to face the issue of class, to become more conscious, to know better so that we can know how best to struggle for economic justice'.

For Christian communities, the first step in tackling the deadly issue of class and classism is facing Christianity's complicity with its construction. We are probably familiar with Christianity's traditional emphasis on charity and care for the poor. We may be more surprised to uncover how Christianity also legitimated over the centuries systems of social, cultural and economic inequality.

In pre-modern centuries, social status was largely fixed and hereditary. The ancient Romans gave birth to the word 'class' (from the Latin *classis*). For the Romans, the term simply categorized who could vote, suffrage being linked to gender, age, land ownership and recourse to militia. The ancient Greek philosophers more formally began categorizing social hierarchies of people. These hierarchies established relations of labour and power, from the 'philosopher king' at the top to the poor at the bottom. The feudal society of the medieval West likewise spoke of 'ranks', 'orders', or 'stations' rather than 'class', but the basic principle of hierarchical division based upon wealth and power remained.

In Christianity, these systems of social stratification became allied with a particular religious way of looking at the world.

The Christian tradition viewed all of creation in relation to the Creator. God created all things, and all things 'participated' or 'shared' in God in their own way. St Paul preached, for example, that in God 'we live and move and have our being' (Acts 17.28). In this participatory vision, medieval Christianity composed what became known as the 'great chain of being'. The 'great chain of being' was a hierarchical concept. It placed God at the top, followed by descending ranks of angels, human-kind, animals, plants, and so on. Everything had its ordained place in the order of things. Things were classified and ranked according to their 'nearness' to God.

The political implications of the great chain of being when it came to human society were obvious. Just as creation involved hierarchical orders, so too were social distinctions ordained by God. Monarchs were at the top as 'God's lieutenants', with descending social ranks beneath them all the way down to the peasants at the bottom. Someone's position in society – and their corresponding wealth, power and status – was part of God's providential ordering of creation. While there were often struggles between nobles and peasants, the underlying theo-logical vision was that of a divinely appointed social hierarchy that legitimated inequalities. Rebellion against masters was also rebellion against God.

The great chain of being shaped religious imaginations and practices, embedding deeply a sense of social hierarchy as divinely appointed. The dominant image that Christianity applied to God was that of lordship and kingship. These imper-ial and regal images were informed by and buttressed the power of the upper classes. Other biblical images of God were elided or held as a minor note. God as a labourer (Gen. 2.4–25), craftsperson (Ps. 19.1), gardener (Ps. 65.9), shepherd (Ps. 23.1), or potter (Rom. 9.21) were displaced by images of lordship. Revolutionary texts that spoke blessing to the poor and woe to those who were rich (Luke 6.20, 24) were sidelined. Texts that envisaged God casting down the mighty and lifting the lowly up (Luke 1.52–53) were spiritualized and set to music through the patronage of those at the top of society. Official prayers often put 'cross' and 'crown' together, conflating religious identity with political obedience to the status quo of hierarchical domination in the name of God.

In this theological mindset, capitalism and mass industrialization emerged, along with the language of 'class'. While the feudal social distinctions slipped away, they were replaced with talk of class distinctions. From there developed social stratifications with which we are still familiar. Capitalism and industrialization radically reconfigured social and economic relations. Class now connected social position explicitly with economics and production. Class became tied to a person's position in manufacture and trade. It was hierarchical in terms of social status but also in relation to wealth and power. The worker was firmly at the bottom of the social hierarchy in every way.

While this modern idea of class suggested the possibility of rising and falling in social position, the reality was more complex. The hierarchy of class quickly entailed oppressive injustice rather than easy social mobility. The working class were looked down upon and kept in poverty.

Class injustice found legitimacy in the thought that emerged around the same time as capitalism and industrialization. The modern concept of class developed at the same time as the Enlightenment ideals of liberty, progress, tolerance and democracy. In relation to class, these soon became empty promises for those in the 'lower' classes.

On the one hand, Enlightenment thought emphasized that social structures were not ordained by God as imagined in the 'great chain of being', but were a human product which changed and evolved over time. Eighteenth-century thinkers such as Jean-Jacques Rousseau, Thomas Paine, and Mary Wollstonecraft advanced the idea that all human beings were created equal. Any social injustice was arbitrary and could be changed.

On the other hand, however, Enlightenment thought also advanced ideas of 'natural' or hereditary 'differences'. These spurious differences were drawn along lines of class, race and gender. Full humanity and human rights were denied to people based upon these characteristics. These supposed 'natural' differences' explained and legitimated poverty and inequality.

Class and classism accordingly became bound up with racism and misogyny. Along with race, class was born out of legitimizing the injustices of capitalism and colonialism. Underpinned by spurious philosophical ideas of natural differences, capitalism and colonialism permitted the 'higher' classes to exploit the 'lower' classes. After all, the superior 'higher' classes deserved a disproportionate share of profits because it was their genius and resources that underpinned production. Likewise, the spurious idea of natural differences also gave permission for racialized violence, plunder and domination across the globe.

Scientific racism proclaimed the fitness of the capitalist class to rule over workers and for whites to rule blacks. As the Indian-born British writer Kenan Malik observes, 'racial divisions had, from the days of colonialism, been created and exploited as a means of fracturing the solidarity of people at the bottom of society, and of derailing political and economic opposition'.[12] The earth and its peoples were the inheritance of those white, male, 'higher' class human beings deemed to be at the apex of society. People became divided according to class, gender and race. They were set against one another to prevent solidarity among the oppressed.

Meanwhile, the theological idea of the 'great chain of being' nevertheless persisted in popular religious discourse. Even after the fall of feudalism and rise of Enlightenment thought, Christian communities often transposed the great chain of being into the language of class. In the popular imagination, the great chain of being and the pseudo-scientific theories of 'natural differences' merged to legitimate the new class distinctions and exploitation.

Two fictional English examples from a rural and an urban context respectively illustrate how the great chain of being continued to legitimate social distinctions and injustices in our modern world.

Lark Rise to Candleford was a trilogy of semi-autobiographical novels by Flora Thompson, published in the 1940s, about the English countryside at the end of the nineteenth century. The trilogy depicted both the charms and the economic precariousness of the rural communities. In one sequence, a local rector appeals to the 'great chain of being' as he teaches the local poor children. The rector quotes from the Catechism that teaches each child to 'order myself lowly and reverently to all betters'. He adjures the children to accept their place in life and acknowledge the right of their social superiors to wealth and power: 'God had placed them just where they were in the social order and given them their own especial work to do; to envy others or to try to change their own lot in life was a sin of which he hoped they would never be guilty.'[13]

The Ragged-Trousered Philanthropists was also a semi-autobiographical novel. Published in 1914, it was written by Robert Noonan under the pen name Robert Tressell. The novel follows a house painter's efforts to find work in a fictional English town and to avoid economic ruin for his family. The novel depicts the hellish realities of such precariousness. It carried the subtitle: 'Being the story of twelve months in Hell, told by one of the damned, and written down by Robert Tressell'. In an early scene, the wife of the protagonist explains to their child what the local clergy have to say about the lot of the precarious worker and the rights of the 'higher' classes: 'The vicar goes about telling [the higher classes] ... that God meant them to have everything that is made by those who work' and that 'God made the poor for the use of the rich'. In turn, she continues, the vicar tells the 'workers' that 'they should be thankful to God' and the rich. Indeed, the workers 'musn't grumble or be discontented because they're poor' as 'God will reward them by letting them go to a place called "heaven"'.[14]

As we can see in the above two examples, the theology of class both legitimated injustice and rendered it as part of a divinely ordained order. The persistence of the great chain of being accordingly often produced what the sociologist Max Weber called the 'theodicy of disprivilege'.[15] In other words, religion explained and justified social inequality and deprivation. Poor people were told they could find compensation for the suffering of their appointed lot in life through charity, a sense of belonging to a religious community, and the promise of heavenly reward in the world to come. It is little wonder that Karl Marx argued that religion was a 'camera obscura' that concealed the causes of oppression and stymied change in the here-and-now.[16]

Christians of all sorts have, of course, always shown concern for those who are less fortunate. Yet this concern is often bound up with different stripes of classism.

On one side, 'conservatives' tend to deal with poverty by encouraging individual improvement and industriousness. Veiled behind this attitude, classism often lurks. Poor people, after all, make their own fate. If they are dependent, they can make choices to escape it. Any failure is their own responsibility.

On another side, 'liberals' tend to develop social programmes to 'lift' people up to the next level. Veiled behind this attitude, classism again often lurks. Poor people need help, and only those in 'higher' classes can save them. Liberals tend towards a form of *noblesse oblige*, the paternalistic notion that those with power and influence must elevate others.

Neither conservatives nor liberals, however, tend to question the very nature of class and its structural injustice. It is easier to imagine the end of the world than the end of exploitative capitalism. Charity soothes symptoms but ignores the deadly disease. Both conservatives and liberals exclude the poor, apart from seeing them as objects of pity and recipients of help. They talk of a 'church *for* the poor' or a 'church *with* the poor'. The poor are never seen as agents of transformation at the heart of the gospel. They are objects of action rather than agents of change. Conservatives and liberals alike lack the idea of a 'church *of* the poor' as forming the heart of the good news. They fail to challenge the fundamental injustice of class and classism that inflects and infects churches and societies.

It does not need to be this way. Just as Christianity has formed part of the problem of class and classism, it also contains radical resources to work towards a different world promised by God.

The idea of a church *of* the poor is central to the movement called 'liberation theology'. Liberation theology describes an approach to practical faithful living focused on social concern for the poor and oppressed. Liberation theology is a modern version of the two ways tradition. It sees freedom from social and economic inequality as integral to the Christian story of salvation. It first emerged in Latin America in the 1960s in the face of extreme economic and political inequality, and has subsequently found global expressions in relation to race and caste as well as to broad social justice through movements such as Black Theology, *Dalit* theology in India, and *Minjung* ['the people'] theology in Korea.

The key idea of Latin American liberation theology is that Christians ought to exercise a 'preferential option for the poor', just as God does in the Scriptures. The Peruvian liberation theologian Gustavo Gutiérrez explains that 'poor' refers to 'victims of material poverty', while 'preferential' means having 'the capacity to accept the will of God in our lives'. Finally, 'option' relates to 'the idea of commitment that ... means solidarity with the poor and rejection of poverty as something contrary to the will of God'.[17] The 'preferential option for the poor' means to give priority to the poor and powerless, as God does.

To join in with God's work, Christians must choose the 'life' offered in a preferential option for the poor and reject all that causes 'death'. The salvation promised by the Christian God encompassed people's material conditions as much as their spiritual state. In Christ, God inaugurated the liberation of people from oppression of every kind. Jesus is the 'liberator', as the Brazilian liberation theologian Leonardo Boff puts it. In Jesus, we see God born, living and dying in poverty and imperial Roman oppression. In Jesus, we see the liberating kingdom of God proclaimed against that grain. In Jesus, we see God victorious over death in all its forms through the resurrection.

'Liberation' is as much a this-worldly reality as it is a spiritual one. The liberation that Jesus brings embodies freedom from poverty and injustice, from all that limits life, and from the selfishness and sin that kills relationship with one another and God. In short, the liberation that Jesus brings means freedom from death and all that causes it. For Boff, Jesus proclaimed the 'kingdom of God', which 'means a total, global, structural revolution of the old order, brought about by God and only by

God'.[18] Liberation begins and ends in God's action; but people of faith join in its unfolding in the messy realities of human communities.

Liberation theology critically reflects upon how Christian practice can align with the liberating will of God in Christ. It calls Christian communities to the two ways tradition of choosing 'life' and opposing 'death'. 'In the final analysis', Gutiérrez writes, 'poverty means death' and is 'a situation that destroys peoples, families, and individuals'. Such deadly poverty is 'institutionalised violence'.[19] In contrast, 'the theology of liberation', writes Gutiérrez elsewhere, 'is an attempt to make present in this world of oppression, injustice and death, the Word of Life'.[20] It is the corporate choice of 'life' over 'death'.

Liberation theology emphasizes the need to analyse the social, economic and cultural causes of class injustice. It gives prominence both to the experience and the voice of working-class struggles for freedom. As the Epistle of James put it, God chooses 'the poor in the world to be rich in faith and to be heirs of the kingdom that he has promised' (James 2.5). Yet liberation theology recognizes that, just like the community to which St James wrote, for too long we 'have dishonoured the poor' and ignored the fact that it is 'the rich who oppress [us]'.

Liberation theology reminds us that any faith that speaks of 'salvation' cannot ignore the historical realities of oppression. Communities of faith must offer liberating alternatives. Neither can faithful communities fail to put the voices of the oppressed at the centre. The starting point of liberation is from the agency of the 'lower' classes and our solidarity with that agency. 'Being poor today', Gutiérrez explains, means 'being involved in the struggle for justice and peace, defending one's life and freedom ... and being committed to the liberation of every human being'.[21] In other words, class consciousness both identifies the roots of class injustice and offers a way to transform social relations for the good of all. We must stand in the critical light of that consciousness and be enlightened by it. As Susan Durber writes, liberation theology recognizes that 'the Christian theological response to "death" must not be burial, or even anointing, but rather resurrection, a change so radical that death itself (poverty itself) is defeated'.[22]

If we are to retrieve a sacred art of contemplating the last thing of death, the agency and voice of the oppressed must be central. That agency and those voices can shape an apocalyptic imagination that unveils the ways in which communities and churches choose 'life' or 'death' in relation to class.

An example of what an apocalyptic imagination sounds like that centres the voice of the working class can be found in one community shaped by liberation theology: Solentiname in Nicaragua during the Somoza dictatorship that ruled the country between 1936 and 1979.

The local population of Solentiname was comprised largely of oppressed *campesinos* or 'peasants'. It was a church *of* the poor. During the latter part of the Somoza dictatorship, liberation theology changed how the local community worshipped. Every Sunday, children would read the Gospel. Instead of a sermon, the worshipping *campesinos* would discuss what they thought about the reading. Working-class voices were at the centre of these Gospel reflections. They read the Gospel through the experience of class oppression. Together, they discerned what kind of response the community might make that worked with the grain of God's righteousness or justice.

From these dialogues, the local Nicaraguan Catholic priest Ernesto Cardenal published *The Gospel in Solentiname* in the late 1970s. That work recorded the conversations of the *campesinos*. The transcribed voices were varied. 'Marcelino was a mystic', wrote Cardenal, 'Rebeca ... always talked about love', while 'Laureano saw everything in terms of the revolution'. 'Elvis was always thinking about the perfect society of the future', continued Cardenal, while 'Felipe ... was constantly aware of the proletarian struggle'. Through these voices and more, Cardenal discerned that 'the true author [was] the Spirit who inspired these comments – the *campesinos* knew very well that it was the Spirit who made them speak'.[23]

One example from *The Gospel in Solentiname* gives a note of what the voice of a church *of* the poor sounds like.[24]

The reading at one meeting was Matthew 26.6–13 (which has parallels in Mark 14.3–9 and John 12.1–8). In that reading, the community heard of how a woman anointed Jesus with expensive ointment ahead of his foretold death. The disciples became angry at her, arguing that 'this ointment could have been sold for a large sum, and the money given to the poor'. Jesus rebuked the disciples. 'You always have the poor with you,' Jesus told them, 'but you will not always have me.'

The community at Solentiname grapple at first with the apparent resignation in this Gospel reading that 'the poor' will always be there. 'This is a phrase', one of them, William, says, 'much used by reactionaries to say there'll always have to be poor people because Christ said so … [and] the world can't change.'

The community also picks up, however, hope in the phrase 'with you' (or 'among you' in their translation). 'As long as there are poor, they will always be among us, we shall not be separated from them,' observes the group. Just as the woman lavishes her loving attention on Jesus, others observe that Christ's followers should do likewise for the poor. We 'have [Christ's] presence in the poor' (cf. Matt. 25.31–46). 'When there's only equality and justice', the conversation continues, then 'Jesus will be with us again.' The way the woman loves Jesus models how his followers must treat the 'poor' and vulnerable among them. Namely, the woman models the loving justice of re-establishing right relations.

One member of the discussion, Olivia, closes this part of the reflection by observing the transformative and demanding character of such love for the poor. Olivia observes that the woman in the story (named as Mary in John's Gospel) looked at Jesus 'like a poor man, a proletarian' and saw that 'he deserved the best there was'. So Mary teaches poor and rich alike. To the poor, she represents total self-giving to one another in love as if we were all little Christs. To the rich, Mary also teaches that 'it's no good to be beating your chest … and not give what you have to the poor'. The 'preferential option for the poor' is absolute in its ethical demand.

The Gospel in Solentiname represents a living out of the 'two ways' tradition reinterpreted by liberation theology. It lets us see what an apocalyptic imagination looks and sounds like. The community reads its own corporate situation through the prism of choosing between 'death' and 'life' under God in Christ the liberator. The church *of* the poor in Solentiname is not an object for others to act upon. The community has its own agency. That agency opens the eyes of all to the deadly realities of class. It has not needed the gospel to be brought to it. It brings the gospel to the world. It advances the hope for a better future. That hope shapes change in the here-and-now.

We desperately need to develop this apocalyptic imagination. We are called to be a church *of* the poor. Our vocation is to live out the two ways tradition and daily choose 'life' in relation to class, especially as it intersects in lethal ways with race and gender.

As we choose life, becoming a church *of* the poor will not simply look like inclusion or celebrating diversity. That would leave the status quo unchallenged. It would not address systemic class inequalities and injustices that kill. Becoming a church *of* the poor means changing churches and the world. The viewpoint and experience of the poor will be the heart of hope and change. Ending poverty will be the living pulse. Christ-like poverty will be the circulation of a new way of life born out of hope. Emptying ourselves of privilege means learning Christ-like poverty that attends 'to the interests of others' as we look for 'life' and reject all that brings 'death' (Phil. 2.1–11).

Choosing life against the deadliness of class will be the locus of God's grace unfolding in our lives and communities. Class solidarity with the oppressed – rather than pity for them – marks this kind of choice. Pope Francis writes in *Evangelii Gaudium* ('The Joy of the Gospel') that such solidarity means 'a new mindset which thinks in terms of community and the priority of the life of all over the appropriation of goods by a few'.[25] For Francis, we must esteem the poor in 'their experience of life, in their culture, and in their ways of living the faith'. Without the 'preferential option for the poor', Francis explains, 'the proclamation of the Gospel ... risks being misunderstood or submerged'. Inequality is the root of social ills. Such inequality kills. As Francis exhorts, 'as long as the problems of the poor are not radically resolved by rejecting the absolute autonomy of markets and financial speculation and by attacking the structural causes of inequality, no solution will be found for the world's problems or, for that matter, to any problems.'

We may feel as if the idol of the market and the structural causes of class inequality are beyond our reach or the influence of our local communities. Cultivating an apocalyptic imagination about death, however, can help us retrieve the two ways tradition that allows us from the grassroots up to choose 'life' and oppose 'death'. Reading the Scriptures through the lens of a preferential option for the poor will transform local churches into churches *of* the poor. The working-class voice and experience can be heard and centred. We can let that voice interrogate how we structure our local churches and worship so that justice is at our heart. We can let that experience help us ask what kind of poverty and inequality exists in our churches and local communities. We can see what we can do when the deadly realities of class around us are laid bare. We can look for practical ways to express 'deep solidarity' with the oppressed, whether in local, national, or international contexts.[26] The intersection between class, race and gender will lead to what the African American activist Angela Davies describes as 'unpredictable or unlikely' coalitions, many of which we may not have dreamt before.[27]

Through the daily choice of 'life' and 'blessing', we can insert hope as a transformative reality into our present social condition of 'death' and 'curse'. It is our working with the grain of God's redemptive purpose. The Holy Spirit moves with the justice inaugurated by Christ. As we step into the flow of that movement, it will, at the end, bring us all into the life of God. Through that Spirit, we can occupy the fullness of the kingdom of heaven.

Notes

1 bell hooks, *Where We Stand: Class Matters*, New York: Routledge, 2000, p. 8.

2 Ambrose, *On His Brother Satyrus*, 2.47, in Edward Condon (ed.), *Death, Judgement, Heaven & Hell*, Washington, DC: The Catholic University of America Press, 2019, p. 2.

3 Augustine, *Sermons of the Liturgical Seasons*, 253.2, in Condon (ed.), *Death, Judgement, Heaven & Hell*, p. 4.

4 Marika Rose, *Theology for the End of the World*, London: SCM Press, 2023, pp. 7–8.

5 Rose, *Theology for the End of the World*, pp. 13–31.

6 Quoted in Alistair Stewart (ed.), *On the Two Ways. Life or Death, Light or Darkness: Foundational Texts in the Tradition*, Yonkers, NY: St Vladimir's Seminary Press, 2011, pp. 14–17.

7 Stewart (ed.), *On the Two Ways*, p. 35.

8 Néstor O. Míguez, 'The Theological Value of Social Class Analysis and Other Social Distinctions' in Joerg Rieger (ed.), *Religion, Theology, and Class: Fresh Engagements after Long Silence*, New York, NY: Palgrave Macmillan, 2013, p. 86.

9 Pierre Bourdieu, *The Social Structures of the Economy*, trans. Chris Turner, Cambridge: Polity Press, 2005, pp. 194–5.

10 Karl Marx and Friedrich Engels, 'Manifesto of the Communist Party' in Karl Marx and Friedrich Engels, *Selected Works*, Moscow: Progress Publishers, 1969, vol. 1, pp. 99–137.

11 Joerg Rieger, 'Introduction: Why Class Matters in Religious Studies and Theology' in Rieger (ed.), *Religion, Theology, and Class*, p. 7.

12 Kenan Malik, *Not So Black and White: A History of Race from White Supremacy to Identity Politics*, London: Hurst, 2023, p. 195.

13 Flora Thompson, *Lark Rise to Candleford*, London: Macmillan, 2020, pp. 212–13.

14 Robert Tressell, *The Ragged Trousered Philanthropists*, Ware: Wordsworth, 2012, p. 101.

15 Max Weber, *The Sociology of Religion*, trans. E. Fischoff, New York, NY: Free Press, 1964.

16 Karl Marx and Friedrich Engels, *The German Ideology*, in *Karl Marx and Frederick Engels – Collected Works*, vol. 5, Moscow and New York, NY: International Publishers, 1976, p. 36.

17 Gustavo Gutiérrez, 'The Task and Content of Liberation Theology' in Christopher Rowland (ed.), *The Cambridge Companion to Liberation Theology*, Cambridge: Cambridge University Press, 2007, p. 27.

18 Leonardo Boff, *Jesus Christ Liberator*, London: SPCK, 1980, pp. 63–4.

19 Gustavo Gutiérrez, *A Theology of Liberation*, Maryknoll, NY: Orbis Books, 1988, p. xxi.

20 Gustavo Gutiérrez, 'The Task and Content of Liberation Theology', in Christopher Rowland (ed.), *The Cambridge Companion to Liberation Theology*, Cambridge: Cambridge University Press, 2007, p. 37.

21 Gutiérrez, *A Theology of Liberation*, p. xxii.

22 Susan Durber, 'A Theology of Poverty' in *Poverty. The Inclusive Church Resource*, London: Darton, Longman & Todd, 2014, p. 79.

23 Ernesto Cardenal, *The Gospel in Solentiname*, Eugene, OR: Wipf and Stock Publishers, 2010, pp. xii–xiii.

24 Cardenal, *The Gospel in Solentiname*, pp. 517–19.

25 Pope Francis, *Evangelii Gaudium*, London: Catholic Truth Society, 2013, p. 95.

26 Joerg Rieger and Kwok Pui-lan, *Occupy Religion: Theology of the Multitude*, Plymouth: Rowman & Littlefield Publishers, 2012, p. 18.

27 Angela Davies, *The Angela Davies Reader*, ed. Joy James, Oxford: Blackwell, 1998, p. 313, quoted in Rieger (ed.), *Religion, Theology, and Class*, p. 202.

Epilogue: Beginnings

If you read history you will find that the Christians who did most for the present world were just those who thought most of the next ... It is since Christians have largely ceased to think of the other world that they have become so ineffective in this. (C. S. Lewis, 1898–1963)[1]

As the Italian poet Cesare Pavese wrote, 'The only joy in the world is to begin.'[2] So, at the close of this little book, we end with a joyful beginning.

We begin every day with a delightful and hope-filled gift of fresh possibility. God in Christ presents the future of the last things as a radical and life-changing offering for the present. The 'future' of the last things erupts into every day with a vision of transformative hope of what could (and will) be. That joyful beginning to every day framed by the last things poses the questions that shape how we view ourselves, what we cherish, where we find our joy and how we act.

How might we begin to let this gift unfold in us and our communities?

How might we begin to live in between the comings of Christ?

How might we begin to attend to the disruptive activity of God such that Christ breaks into our lives today through the Holy Spirit?

This book has attempted to begin some form of response to these sorts of question, offering examples of what it might look like to restore the ancient but nearly lost sacred art of contemplating the last things. This is not simply about retrieving an Advent tradition that we turn to once a year. Contemplating the last things can infuse our daily spiritual practice, from our beginning until our end. It produces an apocalyptic imagination that can shape how we pray, worship, think and act in the world. This allows us to work with the grain of God's grace every day. This apocalyptic imagination allows us to see how the divine Love that moves the sun and other stars also binds together all things in one volume at the end of time. It is a habit and power of seeing the future which God unveils as an explosive reality now. An apocalyptic imagination inspires us with hope to have faith and work in love, even when hope seems futile, or when change feels elusive or illusory. It is imaginative but not imaginary.

Contemplation is not a dispassionate activity divorced from the messiness of life. Contemplation and action reinforce one another in a reflective and reflexive cycle. Contemplation precedes and informs considered action in a complex and ever-changing world. In return, reflecting upon action informs the ongoing work of contemplation that discerns the will of God. Together, the perennial cycle of contemplation and action, shaped by an apocalyptic imagination, unveils how the future promised by God breaks into the here-and-now. It reveals how we can join in that future in our today. An apocalyptic imagination forms a practical and concrete commitment to discerning the movement of God in our lives and communities and to join in with that flow.

This book has linked each of the traditional four last things with a contemporary crisis. These crises were meant to be illustrative rather than restrictive. Indeed, each of the crises might well have been read in light of any of the four last things. Other crises not mentioned could also have been read through an apocalyptic imagination: human sexuality, gender-based discrimination and violence, refugees and mass migration, and human trafficking, to name but a few. This book did not intend to exhaust the possibilities of what an apocalyptic imagination might unveil in the sacred art of contemplating the last things. Beginning that ongoing work of contemplation and action belongs to you, the reader, and your community.

We urgently need to recover this nearly lost sacred art. We have seen how the early Christians placed the last things at the centre of their religious thought and interest. In times of profound crisis, the last things gave a language of hope that informed resilient, realistic and defiantly enduring action. Today, however, the last things languish and are neglected. The decline of the sacred art of contemplating the last things renders us insipid in this life. If we abandon the hope of the last things, we abandon the world in which we live. The radical character of the good news of Christ will be muted in our lives. The last things contain the germ of hope for a better future for which we can strive today in the grace of God.

This vision of hope, however needs two notes of warning. Several chapters have already intimated these warnings, but they are worth repeating.

First, as we cultivate the habit of an apocalyptic imagination, an all-too-easy temptation is to think we are the critical locus of action and change. That is wrong-headed. We, as much as the world, are the subject of what God unveils. God takes the initiative to work within history. We are subject to the winnowing fire of God's scrutiny that seeks the renewal of all creation. An apocalyptic imagination reveals that we and our churches need saving as much as the world. It calls us to humility rather than arrogance, to God's righteousness rather than our own. It calls us to be open to the disruptive action of God in our lives, rather than a close-minded insistence that we are the saviour. The insight of an apocalyptic imagination calls us, in short, to faith, hope and love.

Second, as we deepen in the practice of contemplating the last things, we ought to be wary of sinking into despair. The kingdom of God is not of this world, at least as we know it (John 18.36). The kingdom is 'near' and 'here', but also 'not yet'. When we are faced with cascading crises whose fires conflagrate beyond the contours of what we can see, control or predict, it is easy to give up hope. We should not. God calls us to defiant action against the grain of the world as it is. This defiance anticipates the future that God secures.

Above all, at the end, I hope that retrieving the sacred art of contemplating the last things and developing an apocalyptic imagination will instil a sense of the enticing possibilities we have to join in with God's salvation. Resignation and deferral belong to defeat. We are, however, victors conditioned by humble service born out of love. In this love, Christ is our exemplar, our beginning and end. As St Paul wrote to the Corinthians, therefore, 'thanks be to God, who gives us the victory through our Lord Jesus Christ'.

Notes

1 C. S. Lewis, *Mere Christianity*, San Francisco, CA: Harper, 2001, pp. 134–5.
2 Cesare Pavese, *This Business of Living: Diaries 1935–1950*, London: Transaction Publishers, 2009, p. 55; 23 November 1937.

Questions for Reflection

These questions are designed for individual or group use to help you reflect upon each chapter. They are not exhaustive but are offered as one tool to help cultivate a daily apocalyptic imagination about the last things in your life.

Introduction: Endings

1. What do you typically associate with the season of Advent?
2. What do you make of the centrality of the four last things in much of the Christian contemplative tradition?
3. What do the four last things of heaven, hell, death and judgement immediately evoke for you?
4. How do you react to modern suspicions about the four last things as superstitious relics?
5. What do you make of the idea of cultivating an 'apocalyptic imagination' about the four last things to create a vision of hope?
6. What surprised you the most in this chapter and what hope do you take away from it?

1 Heaven

1. What do you typically associate with the word 'heaven' and how do you feel about it?
2. What do you make of the biblical idea that the 'earth' and 'heaven' form one integrated whole?

3. What does the 'kingdom of heaven' look like and mean to you?
4. What do you think about the claim that 'heaven' both poses a problem and offers a resource to think about our environmental crisis?
5. How do the creation stories of Genesis 1 and Revelation 21 shape your attitudes and practices in relation to the earth and its peoples?
6. What surprised you the most in this chapter and what hope do you take away from it?

2 Hell

1. What do you typically associate with the word 'hell' and how do you feel about it?
2. What do you make of the biblical images, described in this chapter, sometimes translated as 'hell'?
3. Does God's saving will to 'reconcile all things to himself' (Col. 1.19) change what and how you think about 'hell'?
4. What do you think about the claim that 'hell' diagnoses this-worldly ills and calls us to join in with God in dismantling 'hell'?
5. How does the idea that 'hell' describes spiritual alienation from God and one another enlighten social crises like populism?
6. What surprised you the most in this chapter and what hope do you take away from it?

3 Judgement

1. What do you typically associate with the word 'judgement' and how do you feel about it?
2. To what extent do you agree that the Bible is concerned with 'judgement' insofar as it calls us to be concerned with justice?

3. In what ways do you think that Jesus embodies divine justice and offers us a 'ministerial vision' of right relations?
4. In what ways does the idea of 'judgement' as 'justice' help you think about the crisis of racial injustice?
5. What did you find interesting and what did you find challenging about Black theology as a resource to develop an apocalyptic imagination about 'judgement'?
6. What surprised you the most in this chapter and what hope do you take away from it?

4 Death

1. What does the word 'death' evoke for you and how do you feel about it?
2. What do you make of the 'two ways' tradition in terms of thinking about 'death'?
3. In what ways do you experience and understand 'class' and 'classism' as deadly realities?
4. What do you make of the idea of a 'preferential option for the poor' and what might it mean for you and your community?
5. What does the example of The Gospel in Solentiname speak into your community?
6. What surprised you the most in this chapter and what hope do you take away from it?

Epilogue: Beginnings

1. What do you now think about the sacred art of contemplating the last things?
2. How have you been shaped by exploring the idea of developing an 'apocalyptic imagination'?
3. What changes to your life and faith are you taking away from this book?

www.ingramcontent.com/pod-product-compliance
Lightning Source LLC
Chambersburg PA
CBHW030257231224
19395CB00004B/27

9 781786 225658